IF YOU'R
OR AN O

A note on the photography and drawings

The illustrations in *Two Wheel Travel* come from a variety of sources. Children in Vermont elementary schools, Elaine Alberga and Chris Kluge, have added their own particular marks to this book just for the fun of it. Stephen Robeck has taken most of the photographs that you'll find here, but Syd and David Greenberg have also contributed to this book's illustrations. The manufacturers of a number of parts have given us photographs and line drawings, and we are grateful for their help.

The pictures that are simply here for the fun of it aren't always like those found in touring books and magazines. You'll find few machines propped in front of woods and hills. This is because we've made an effort to reproduce something of the visual effect of touring with these photographs. You know that when you ride you rarely see other bikes. You only park yours in order to stop and look at it and perhaps take a picture. The touring, though, is a matter of scenes that contain only people and things along the way. So, many of our photographs are simply that sort of thing.

TWO ○ WHEEL ○ TRAVEL
Bicycle
CAMPING AND TOURING

Condensed from the Bestseller

PETER TOBEY, Editor

A DELL BOOK

Published by
DELL PUBLISHING CO., INC.
1 Dag Hammarskjold Plaza
New York, New York 10017

CONTENTS

BICYCLING

RIDING TECHNIQUES OF LONG-DISTANCE CYCLING: A careful look at the way your body performs and reacts to miles of cycling. Some thoughts on technique to keep you comfortable and moving. *By Peter Braddock* **Page 18**

BICYCLE SOCIETIES AND ASSOCIATIONS: Brief outlines of some of the interested groups in the world of touring. **Page 34**

BICYCLE CARRIERS: All about loading bicycles on cars. There are a couple of plans from 'Chick' Mead for rooftop carriers you can make yourself. **Page 45**

EUROPEAN CYCLE TOURING: If you're going abroad, don't see Europe by train. An introduction to touring there, and some remarks on bicycling in several countries. *By Peter Knottley* **Page 54**

MAGAZINE AND BOOK REVIEWS: There's lots of good reading on the newstands and in the library. **Page 75**

BICYCLES

THE POWER TRAIN: An introduction to the workings of derailleurs and a thorough study of the available models. There's a section on touring derailleurs and their capacities that will help you outfit your machine. *By Robert Drennan*   **Page 86**

GEARS—A LITTLE TEN-SPEED THEORY: Choosing from among the many combinations of gear ratios is often an unknown and always a complex problem. This is a straightforward introduction to ratio theory and what it means on the road. *By Richard B. Terry* **Page 130**

CARRYING THE LOAD: Some deadweight theory that every camping cyclist should know about and a wish book of the very finest panniers and bags. *By William Yeuf*   **Page 142**

WHAT TIRES FOR TOURING?: All about picking and fixing rims and tires for touring. *By Richard B. Terry*   **Page 155**

BRAKES: The how and why of choosing a stopper. *By Robert Drennan*   **Page 171**

CAMPING

TENTS: A study of the equipment available and a discussion of how to choose from among all these shelters. *By James Fuller*   **Page 188**

LESS-THAN-TENT-ROOFS: If you can't afford or don't want to carry a backpacking tent, these makeshift shelters may fit your needs on the road.   **Page 206**

SLEEPING BAGS: There's more to these envelopes than meets the eye, and what you don't see is what you ought to know before you buy one. This article contains a chart of all the lightweight bags suitable for touring. *By Peter W. Tobey*   **Page 226**

CAMPING AND SURVIVAL BOOK REVIEWS: One review and a few suggestions that will help once you get off the bike and into camp.   **Page 252**

LIGHTWEIGHT FOODS: Any food you carry with you has to be light and keep well on the road. Provisions for a tour go well beyond jerky and canned goods and this article takes a look at a wide variety of them. There's even a short cookbook included.   **Page 263**

CAMPING EQUIPMENT SUPPLIERS: An editorialized listing of the mail-order and retail outlets for high quality and inexpensive camping gear.   **Page 283**

INTRODUCTION

Bicycling isn't much like anything else. It has its similarities with walking and running and even with mountaineering, but as a sport it's unique. The feeling and discipline of pedaling yourself on an incredibly efficient and simple machine one hundred miles isn't quite like any other. The even movements, the constant and controlled effort, and the skill of traveling under your own power constitutes about as satisfying a sport as any.

Bicycling's a simple thing to do. But, at the same time, the techniques and understandings that go into touring at its best are many and complex. The thrill doesn't come from danger or speed or even extreme exertion, but rather from a controlled and disciplined effort. As a result, bicycling at its best is a very measured, even moderated sport that is best enjoyed only when it's gone at consistently.

Recreational touring and camping doesn't require the furthest reaches of effort that racing demands. The margin for error is wider and the critical concerns of time are almost unimportant. But the tourist is very much involved with the speed and control of his bike. He, like the racer, knows by his own system of grades and marks if the whole thing has been well carried off. You can, of course, get sore legs and tired arms by committing some error, but a fit and practiced cyclist can learn to avoid that sort of failing. He can ride all day, locked into his machine, controlling it and himself, and won't by any means feel hurt.

But if this pleasure is the result of a science, it's one that is different from the racer's. The tourist doesn't live on the ragged edge of dumping his machine. He isn't pressed for every bit of speed because there's no prize for getting there three minutes early. Much more is the fact that his discipline, his concentration, is caught up in doing it all well. And in doing it well over and over again.

Perhaps it's this long-term and autonomous involvement that separates the camping cyclist from racers and around-town bikers. A tour is a whole thing, a unit, and going about it day after day gives you a special sort of satisfaction. In effect, the tourist loads everything he needs into a few cubic feet and leaves. As long as he is traveling he is more or less isolated from easy sources of assistance and so has to maintain himself, his machine, and all his gear. Tending to the business of a trip isn't a matter of survival so much as it is of measured accomplishment. Although a rider isn't always lost in the wilderness, he does make himself responsible for all of his small, mobile world. It's his strength that turns those miles. He exercises a wide variety of skills on and off the bike, day after day, and if he is good at it he manages in both a relaxed and concentrated way. Although he may not break any records, the challenge of the sport is still there.

I take my fleeing seriously. It's a kind of Pooh Bear adventure, vicarious, controlled, and good humoured, but still I like going to see the country. I like being physically close to the place I'm traveling through. I really enjoy concentrating on my bike and gear, on camping techniques and food and rain, to the exclusion of less important matters. I like to run away even if I have to admit that pretty soon I'll turn around and go back to work. It's a little demanding and sort of trivial, and some people say that it's a phase I'm going through, that I'll soon have it out of my system. But I enjoy thinking about and practicing all the aspects of camping and cycling. I like the riding and the work and I like the problems that have to be solved so that things won't go too wrong.

A number of us who enjoy traveling on precarious vehicles have compiled this 'how-to' manual to deal with some of the problems and solutions involved in camping and touring. Most of us are both motorcyclists as well as bicyclists and feel that the skills of each sport can be added to each other. As a result, you'll find we want to offer you some information on the sports of walking and motorcycling in order to give you some advice on bicycle touring. We deal with things that are generally true of bicycling and with problems that are peculiar to touring.

You can skim those few remarks that are devoted to motorcycles, but there are some interesting and useful parallels between the two sports that you can gain from. Those articles that relate to both two-wheel sports have been published in a motorcycle book very much like this one. If you find them offensive, let us know about it.

Another unusual characteristic of this book is that it doesn't spend most of its time talking about bicycles. There are, of course, articles on some bikes, and rundowns on their particular components, but this book focuses on touring. It covers some of the accessories and gear for your bike that we feel are important on the road. It also deals with some camping equipment and techniques. Information about maps and credit cards just seem to us to relate to these topics. Much of the gear that is discussed here wasn't intended for those of us who bicycle but it can be very easily appropriated for our purposes. We've just taken information from anywhere we could in order to add to your knowledge of the comfort and safety of touring.

The sum of these articles will give you a cross-section of most of the important components of a camping and touring system. It is by no means complete. The point is that rather than look at the individual machines and their relative merits as a full-time job, we've tried to begin studying a large range of equipment that ought to go into a long tour. More important, this is a text that covers a wide scope of considerations that you should think about and practice when you're on the road. These pages are not about the things that other people do; they are about what you can do. There are no travelogues, no reports on tours or races. This is a strictly 'how-to' book.

A bicycle mechanic may well be able to get himself and his machine from one side of this continent to the other, but he may have a miserable time doing so. Choosing a tent and sleeping bag, preparing meals and outfitting your bike to tour are all problems that deserve careful consideration. In fact, they demand it.

The more you regard touring in this light, the more your attitude toward a long ride changes and develops. The camping bicyclist has to think about a rather complex system. Simple, compact, and light it may well be, but it is also filled with potential for malfunction and misuse. As a result, the cyclist should choose his gear and maintain it so that it will remain efficient. The cleaner the works, the better and longer they'll run. After you've chosen your stuff, you should treat it with the same respect you do your machine because you rely on all of it. Finally, you have to understand the foibles of what can happen to you off the bike as well as on it.

Most long-distance tourists are cyclists who have decided to pack up and take a long ride. Some are more expert than others at the camping aspects of their ride, but most employ techniques that leave something to be desired. Their equipment is often a hand-me-down collection from the world of station-wagon weekends in the national park system. They take their bikes and put up with the camping because it's the only cheap way to go.

The trouble is that this sort of rider is missing much

that his tour might include. There is something very satisfying to be had from a bicycle ride that involves a lot of camping. There is the extreme of bicycling's autonomy and freedom and there is the additional pleasure of seeing the country and of controlling your machine.

Putting the whole system together can be a lot of fun. Even if you haven't the money for the best, you can improvise effective equipment and make the whole thing work. You can understand it all and use it well with only a little practice and care. Mastering a complete, self-contained and self-propelled system is one of the most satisfying dimensions of bicycling. If you work at it, you can achieve an intelligent and measured performance that will make your trip. That, I guess, is what we mean by 'retreat gracefully.'

If everything works the way it ought to, you won't be bothered with details. If you're not caught up in the trivia of traveling, then perhaps, as you pass through Fenario, you'll recognize it.

P. W. T.

BICYCLING

RIDING TECHNIQUES OF LONG DISTANCE CYCLING

by Peter Braddock

Using your bicycle for Saturday afternoon sport or for errands is good fun and moderate exercise. But it doesn't require great physical conditioning nor careful consideration of how your muscles move you and your bike mile after mile. Even an ambitious weekend tour involves much more critical efficiency than does short, around the block riding. Errors of judgment and mistakes in technique lead, with time, to an accumulation of physical problems that can be unforgivable on a long ride. It's therefore essential to use what resources you have in the most consistently efficient way if you want to enjoy yourself through the whole trip and get to where you're going in good shape.

In fact, consistency itself is one of the most important parts of cycling efficiency. This is so for the

simple reason that the body maintains itself in a balanced, patterned manner. To effectively use what it can produce you must draw from your body in an analogously balanced and patterned way.

Both respiration and blood flow operate in an interconnected, rhythmic fashion. These processes supply muscles with nourishment and oxygen while simultaneously removing metabolic waste. Any physical exertion which is to be sustained over a long period of time must operate within the limits of the body's systems. That is, you can only pedal within the limitations of your body's ability to supply energy. Your cycling must be geared to that pace.

Cadence is pedaling at a rhythmic, constant pace; it is the timing of crank revolutions to the consistent rate of the body's metabolism. After all, pedaling is the major output, the product of your body's exertion, and the idea behind cadence simply recognizes that there is an ideal pace at which you can create energy and expend it.

Going too slow is one way of varying from that ideal timing. In the first place it is clearly inefficient: You're simply not using all the energy available to move the bicycle. What's more, sustaining a consistent cadence depends in large part on your feeling locked into it. Once you've got a really clear, effective sense of the propriety of your proper pace, believe me you *know* it. It is just this feeling of true cadence that enables you to maintain crank revolutions at a constant pace. Going too slow fogs that certainty and as a result you may oscillate your pedaling speeds. First you pedal very slowly and then accelerate, then you go slightly slower again and then once again quicken your pace until you soon begin to tire yourself.

But, more often than actually tiring yourself, you begin to feel sluggish after pedaling a while at too slow a pace, and you mistake this lethargy for real weariness. You feel as though maybe yesterday or the day before you exerted yourself too much when you really haven't. But, the fact remains that the next big hill looks just as insurmountable as it does when you're really exhausted.

If too slow a pace is inefficient, too fast a pace will be debilitating. Because your metabolism is balanced within certain limits of exertion, pushing too fast simply accumulates wastes and exhausts your supply of energy. You're taxing your body beyond the level that it can maintain. It is true that you will usually adjust to the temporary demands of extra effort, but you cannot sustain that level over the long periods necessary for touring. The physical balance supporting your natural cadence is upset, reserves of energy are depleted and getting back into your groove may be hard without a considerable amount of rest.

There's also more to this matter than the relatively short-term exhaustion of your energy. Being tired is only one symptom of overtaxing your body. There are others that can be even more important. Wear and strain on muscles, ligaments, and joints are cumulative if you have to keep going and they'll slow you and eventually make your whole endeavor painfully impossible.

Therefore, a prime concern must be to eliminate to as great a degree as possible the pitfalls which accompany either too fast or too slow a cadence. This is done by discovering, establishing, and cultivating a technique of pedaling which reflects the ongoing metabolic rate of your body. How then, do you find this natural pace or cadence? Forty miles of conscientiously trying will probably do it, but for a start follow this method. Count your number of heartbeats while at rest for one minute. Exercise mildly for several minutes and then count your number of heartbeats for the ten seconds immediately afterwards. After another thirty seconds of rest count again for one minute. If the first and last count are not very close in number, do the whole thing over, starting again from rest. This time exercise more mildly so that you recover more quickly and your final count more closely matches your initial one while at rest.

How fast your heart recovers completely from exercising tells you something about how much you're taxing your body. Most important is the fact that recovery from any given amount of work is relative to how fit you are. If you're in poor shape, relatively mild exertion will overwork your muscles and wastes will build up in them. The fact that your heart rate does not recover quickly simply indicates that it is working to clear those wastes and resupply the tissues with oxygen. Any level of exertion that develops this backlog or debt in muscle tissue cannot be sustained over a long period of time. Your muscles will just stop working.

So, if you find a level of activity by mild exercising from which you can recover very quickly, you will also have found a pace that you can reasonably maintain for long periods. If the first and last count are virtually the same, multiply the ten-second count you made immediately after exercising by six to compute, roughly, heartbeats per minute. This rate reflects your manageable limit of exertion.

What you have done is taken an index, an arbitrary measure of your heart in a balanced state of exertion. Since your heart works in concert with respiration and other bodily functions, this is a measure of your whole body in such a balanced state.

Now, the next step is to get on your bike and search for a low gear in which you can smoothly pedal a number of crank revolutions per minute which is approximately the average of the number of your heart-beats while resting and while exercising mildly. Again, do this for several minutes and make sure you can recover quickly. If not, try a lower gear. If you do recover quickly consider the pace close to your natural cadence in a gear appropriate to flat terrain (and avoid hills at first).

As you get into better shape your cadence will increase as will your number of heartbeats per minute while you are exercising comfortably. You will also be able to push harder on the pedal with each revolution and still be comfortable, i.e., you'll begin to use slightly higher gears for the same terrain. But, your body will recover at the same rate. If it does not, you will loose the feeling of freshness that comes from being locked into your natural cadence and you will overtax yourself.

You must be sensitive to the development of your strength and endurance and not push your cadence too high or too fast or stay too long in too high a gear. The best way to keep from doing this is to learn and come to sense how you feel when you *know* your cadence is correct. Cultivate sensing that feeling and try to keep it with you while you ride, whatever the conditions.

Unfortunately, varying conditions make cadence, once established, difficult to maintain mile after mile. Changing terrain and weather conditions place demands upon any rider to vary the speed and force of the pedaling motion. You shouldn't allow this to happen. Instead, learn to select the proper gears for such a change in condition, at the proper time, and continue pedaling at a consistent pace. All this takes knowledge of ten- or fifteen-speed gearing or both and a good deal of practice. That knowledge comes in the form of planning so that you select the most suitable gear arrangement for the weather and terrain you expect to encounter on your trip. Practice so that you can shift smoothly into the appropriate gear without brakes in the rhythm of your cadence.

While maintenance of a consistent cadence is central to efficient pedaling, it does not cover all of that story. With practice, you can put more muscles to work and pedal more smoothly. Ankling is a technique whereby you use your foot as a lever with your ankle as a fulcrum while pedaling on the ball of your foot. It enhances the speed of the down and up stroke as well as giving the pedal motion a boost through dead center areas. There is a correct way to ankle and as this is the most efficient way to do it, you should take time to learn how so it comes smoothly and without concentration.

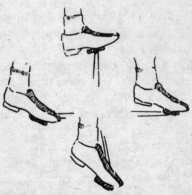

Be especially careful to place your foot properly on the pedal with the ball directly over the pedal spindle. This insures the proper lever action. This technique puts to work many of the muscles used in walking that would go unexercised if you tried to pedal with your heel. You can simulate that by holding your calf while you push down on the floor with your foot relaxed. Now hold your calf and push with your leg and ankle, centering your force on the ball of your foot.

While learning the technique itself, ride in a place where you can watch the motion of your feet without fear of having an accident—possibly in a large, empty parking lot. Expect to be more conditioned for pushing down with your toe than pulling up. This pulling up motion isn't used in walking so you won't immediately be fit for much of it. Generally, this lifting should be kept to a minimum at first until your muscles begin to get used to that action.

The key to ankling effectively is smoothness. If you are unable to ankle correctly in a smooth fashion, develop your own pedaling motion making sure it is an uninterrupted flow. It's more important to be smooth through the full arc of the crank's revolution than to unevenly execute a strict ankling motion.

A consistent cadence and smooth ankling motion form the necessary groundwork for efficient cycling. They are a foundation upon which a variety of riding techniques and body positions can be combined to suit varying conditions. The weather and terrain can not only cause more or less difficulty but certain muscles

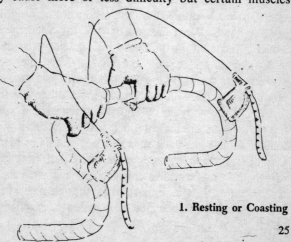

1. Resting or Coasting

and joints can get periodically tired. Variety is crucial. It allows you to be consistent in your rhythm even as big hills or wind tend to change it. Variation in technique and style also enables the cyclist to put varying conditions to his best advantage as well as minimizing any disadvantage that arises.

The points of bodily contact on a bicycle are the handlebars, seat, and pedals. The biker can, by varying his grip on the bars, shifting his seat on the saddle and his foot position on the pedals, alter his total posture on the bike. He can, therefore, change what muscles are doing what work as well as adapt to the external conditions of weather and terrain.

There are five basic hand positions on the 'Maes' bar. All have advantages and disadvantages in terms of certain conditions. I've given them names just to associate them with the sorts of situations they are best suited to.

Figure 1 represents the 'resting or coasting' position. Putting your hands on the tops of the bars places your body in its most upright posture and so it provides relief to a tired back or neck. Shifting your weight to a more vertical position distributes more of it on the seat. Obviously, this action will take a lot of weight off of your hands. What pressure is still supported by your hands is centered on the fleshy area between the thumb and index finger, a welcome change from the steady pressure on the ball of your hand which is the main point of contact with the bar in most other positions.

With the body so upright riding with the hands on top of the bars is efficient when you are moving with a strong wind. Your back acts as a sail and helps to push you along. Don't underestimate the wind. Regardless of whether it's working for you or against you, accommodating it is as important as shifting gears before climbing a hill. This hands up position is excellent for coasting down hill as well. It affords maximum wind resistance and so avoids your having to use the brakes frequently.

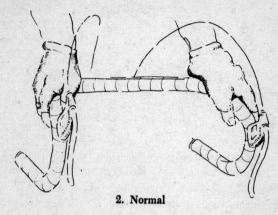

2. Normal

The 'normal' handgrip is illustrated in figure 2. This is the position which seems to be preferred by the average cyclist. It is balanced, with your weight distributed between your hands and seat. The arc of your body is a cross between its form in the upright and down position (see figure 5). As in the case of the upright grip, the shoulders have a tendency to stay put and not to move with the pedaling motion. If your shoulders do move slightly there is a mixture of both horizontally and vertically directed force. With such a balanced form, this 'normal' position is not suited to any one job but adequate for cruising over moderately diverse terrain.

Figure 3 is the 'forward' position in which the body is thrown the farthest forward as the result of a handgrip. Because the body is arched far forward the back and abdomen muscles are used to a great extent. There is a tendency for the arms to pull at the brakes, creating a horizontal shoulder movement. This pulling

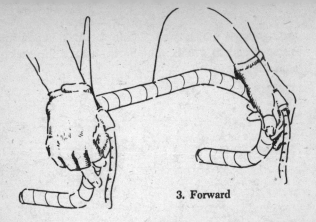

3. Forward

and pushing forward coupled with the involvement of the larger, durable back and abdomen muscles makes the position a good one for high speed riding on flat land. It is a very strong posture and, as long as the wind is not a significant factor, it will really move you along.

Riding forward is also an excellent way of resting your hands. Again, the pressure is off the ball of the hand and placed on the fleshy portion between the thumb and forefinger. Another plus is that the effects of any added pressure, which results from the body's forward tilt, is easily absorbed by the rubber brake covering.

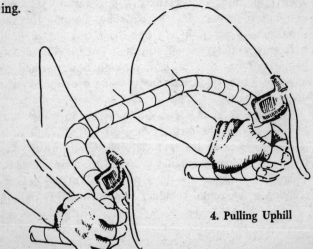

4. Pulling Uphill

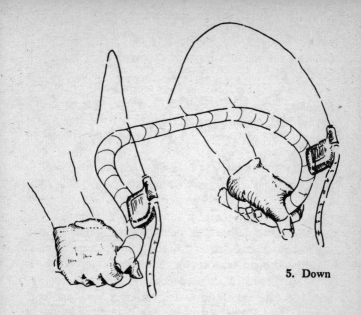

5. Down

In figure 4, 'pulling uphill', the body is thrown both forward and down. There is a tendency to pull with the arms, creating a diagonal shoulder movement. Your body is streamlined, approaching the very efficient 'C' created by the 'down' position. This is definitely the work posture for climbing hills. Your arms are in a position to pull, with the shoulders moving diagonally into the slope of the hill. This position forces an alternating pushing and pulling action on the part of the back and abdomen. Your body is also streamlined for a low profile to cut wind resistance. This low profile makes the 'pulling uphill' handgrip excellent as well for pulling downhill or against the wind.

Figure 5, the 'down' position, is an extremely efficient one and a comfortable one, too, once you adapt the necessary muscles. Your back is stretched and your stomach and abdomen contracted. Your neck is bent to its greatest degree, which may take some getting used to. But the totality of the position is so efficient and eventually comfortable that it is a small price to pay.

Since your palms face the ground and your arms pull and push almost vertically, there is a tendency toward up and down movement. Your shoulders will rise and fall and your legs will pump almost straight up and down.

Here, your body is in a tight 'C' arc from seat to bars and, like a spring, your muscles work in an unbroken line from hand to foot. This is another work position, best for moving into the wind as a result of its extra low profile. The fact that arm, shoulder and leg force is vertical helps to minimize its direct conflict with the straight on force of the wind.

These five basic hand positions help the body to adapt to internal strain and a variety of external conditions. But, they represent only basic tools to be altered and shaped to one's own particular needs. Experiment with combinations of the five. For instance, the combination of the left hand in figure 1 and the right hand from either figure 4 or 5 relaxes the back and is efficient for winds coming from a variety of directions. Drop a shoulder into a wind coming from one side and toward you or set it as a sail when there is any push from behind.

Hand positions which force the body forward tend to create horizontal pushing and pulling forces. This action is suited to flatter terrain and riding with the wind. Positions which throw the body down enhance vertical movement. Thinking about positioning as effecting horizontal and vertical thrust is a distinction that is made just to demonstrate how various grips work. Don't take them strictly. The movements of your body while pedaling in any position are a combination of both. What's being said here is an effort to draw your attention to dominant tendencies so you can use them to best advantage.

Not only is movement important in moving the bike on a variety of terrains but position also affects what particular muscles you use most. Positions higher on the bars relax the neck, stretch the stomach and ease the back and hands. Down positions do the opposite, stretching the back and contracting the stomach while using your hands and arms to the fullest. Think about the muscles being used and not being used in any particular position. Try to invent ways to relax those that get tired quickest and to employ those that play too small a part in other postures. If you think about it and cultivate a sensitivity to what's going on with your body, you'll be able to use all the muscles available to move the bike and also be able to work with them as much or as little as they will support you comfortably.

The position of a rider on the seat is governed, to some extent, by the position of his hands and the corresponding tendency to a certain shoulder movement. If the shoulder movement is horizontal, the total forward push on the bicycle may be enhanced from time to time by sliding to and fro on the saddle. Do this rhythmically, in time with the shoulders and arms and, of course, in time with the pedaling motion. Such movement is thus directed to both forward and down. Down in the sense that the body's weight follows the pedal from its twelve o'clock to a six o'clock position and is directly overhead throughout that arc. Keeping your weight directly over the pedal takes some of the pressure off the leg muscles. This sliding motion also relieves a buildup of heat and sweat in the groin area, but it may lead to chafing if the rider doesn't wear chamois covered or similarly friction-free bicycle pants.

The other seat position is to rise off the saddle

itself. Again, this stance keeps the sweat down, especially on downhill runs where it provides good air circulation. On such a downhill ride, bringing the seat off of the saddle levels the body more, lessening the wind resistance and maximizing speed.

The only other time you might lift your seat completely is when you're pulling hard uphill. I'd like to discourage this technique for the tourer. It is not inefficient per se, but it uses so much energy so fast that it is generally inefficient on a long day's ride.

There is one further word in regard to seat position. Any stance you might dream up will be uncomfortable if the saddle is not broken in correctly. Doing this right takes about four hundred miles of riding plus *light* oiling from underneath *only once*. The seat has to hold its shape in order to remain comfortable and that means keeping it dry all the time. Put a shower cap over it in the rain.

Foot positions are limited as a result of the somewhat strictly defined motion of pedaling. But there are alternatives to ankling. You can pedal in a straight up and down motion. This is much less efficient but is very good for some leg and foot strains.

One such position is to point your toe down all the way through the 360° revolution of pedaling. Push from the thigh, locking the calf, ankle joint, and foot into one unflexing piece. This action does a great deal to relieve tiring lower leg muscles but you should use the technique only toward that end.

Another position is to point the toe straight up throughout the pedaling sequence. This stretches and relaxes the calf.

If you do not wear cleats, you may try another series of foot positions. Taking care to keep the foot in proper position on the pedal, you may rotate the foot. From bird's eye view, simply turn your heel clockwise or counterclockwise just slightly. This spreads the stress and work out in differing amounts among the muscles on the outer and inner side of the lower leg. At the same time the knee can be pointed slightly out or in, changing the configuration of upper leg muscles doing the work. Do this only sparingly, however, as you may damage your knees as a result.

In fact, you should be conscious that any variation from the most strictly efficient positions is to be used only in order to employ different muscles while relaxing those that generally do the work. Any time you intend to cycle on a long tour you have to think in terms of the most efficient way of using what strength you have. You have to conserve your energy and deal it out to the road in measured amounts. But to do that best doesn't mean cycling in a fixed position all the time. A technique that you use only temporarily may be a long-term benefit even if it is less efficient while you're using it.

The key is to vary your position to suit your body's needs and the requirements of the weather and terrain. But remember that one of your primary needs is to be consistent in your timing even as you vary your body's posture and pedaling techniques.

Finally, experiment. Cultivate sensitivities to what you're using to get the job done and try ways of shifting responsibilities now and then. A few minutes of what might seem wasteful and awkward change can bring relief to parts of you that should be exerting themselves optimally for greatest long-term efficiency. ●

BICYCLE SOCIETIES

American Youth Hostels, Inc.

American Youth Hostels is a nonprofit association that is organized to encourage simple, inexpensive travel and outdoors activity. AYH sports include bicycling, hiking, skiing, sailing, and canoeing, all of which are strung together by the system of Youth Hostels around the world.

AYH members and passholders may stay in any of the 4,200 hostels found in forty-seven countries. These are very simple, overnight accommodations that, ideally, are located in the most scenic, historical, and cultural areas of each member country. In fact, the system is extensive in places where people are willing to 'parent' a hostel. In many European countries, though not so much in the U.S., the network of hostels is extensive and travel that relies solely upon them for evening stopovers is possible. So far, there are only 102 hostels in the U.S. and 40 in Canada.

A Youth Hostel in the U.S. can be a school, church,

AND ASSOCIATIONS

donated roof of any decent kind or, in some cases, a specially built facility; abroad, just about everything is commandeered: old ships and castles have been converted and there is a string of mountain, ski lodge hostels. Overnight fees range from 40¢ to $1.25 abroad and $1.50 to $2.00 in this country and Canada.

The touring bicyclist can find a wide variety of foreign and domestic trips sponsored by the AYH. The travel department of the AYH national headquarters plans over fifty hosteling tours each summer. They last as long as six weeks and local, one and two day jaunts are also sponsored by individual city councils. The longer rides cost from $240.00 to $1100.00, which covers food, lodging and an experienced leader.

All the tours are rated in terms of difficulty, but the easiest isn't easy. The pedaling covers a lot of ground and the accommodations aren't to be mistaken for luxury, but this is a safe, inexpensive way to see lots of country. The AYH has a pamphlet outlining their tours, which use bicycles, Volkswagen buses and public transportation in differing proportions. As an example of what AYH offers the bicyclist who likes his camping is this trip:

The Great River Run lasts thirty-six days, costs $305.00, begins in St. Paul, Minnesota and ends in Chicago, Illinois. The tour goes through Minnesota, Wisconsin, Iowa, and Illinois and follows a long stretch of the Mississippi. Sixty percent of the days rely on camping accommodations. This one is rated A-B, which means the pedaling varies from the challenging sort to a bunch of fifty-sub-fifty mile days.

There are a few requirements and some 'Hosteling Customs' that may tell you if this is your kind of overnight. A sleeping bag, or a couple of nylon sheets and a pillow, and your own eating utensils are required. You should arrive at the hostel between 4:00 and 7:00 P.M. and lights out is at 10:00 P.M. No smoking, drinking, or using illegal drugs is permitted.

Hosteling is defined by the association as traveling under your own power. This includes a number of special circumstances and exceptions and you can arrive at the first hostel with an engine under you, but that's the end of it. "Traveling under your own power" isn't really what they mean, or at least that definition seems strained to me. Bicycling and hiking certainly fill the bill, but horseback riding is also included in the acceptable modes of getting from one place to another. The AYH sponsors Volkswagen trips but won't let you hitchhike, indeed, they prohibit it in capital letters. If you arrive on a motorcycle, regardless of how well the exhaust is muffled and even if you have the staid addition of a magnificent sidecar with your mother in it, you'll be turned away.

The AYH has a number of fine books and pamphlets

BIKE ROUTE

they sell at reasonable cost and they also supply, through the mail, some very good bicycle gear. You'll find some of their stuff reviewed elsewhere in here. If you'd like further information, applications for membership and the like, write to their national headquarters. The AYH hosteling flyer lists all of the local offices and their addresses.

American Youth Hostels, Inc.
20 West 17th Street
New York, New York   10011

The International Bicycle Touring Society

The International Bicycle Touring Society had a humble beginning that has affected the casual and friendly way in which it has operated ever since. In 1964 Clifford Graves, a California surgeon who loved to pedal, organized a tour of New England with a bunch of friends. A very limited amount of publicity in small-circulation magazines followed but a surprising number of tourists showed up for the ride. They came from all walks of life and were every age and, in short, had a good time. Before they disbanded, they formed the society and dubbed themselves 'Huff-and-Puffers'. The thing has grown ever since.

The IBTS isn't a privately owned, profit making operation. Doctor Graves handles the mail and the members work on the tours. It's an all volunteer effort.

Somebody with a little experience decides that he knows a good area close to his home and so he lays out a route, picks the hotels, and notifies the IBTS. The tour is announced. People write for information and correspondence begins, either handled by the central office or the tour's leader. Regardless, the leader donates a lot of his time and isn't paid for anything more than out-of-pocket expenses while he's planning and organizing the ride. When it comes to the tour, he pays his way like everybody else.

Because the volunteer leader does what he can, there is little of the complaint and tourist irritability found on lots of tours. Details mess up now and then and everyone generally enjoys himself.

These aren't camping tours. Huge panniers and camping gear aren't carried because nobody camps. Extra gear of any kind is hauled by a 'sag wagon,' a following car that is a constant feature of huff-and-puff tours, and sometimes a rider, over his head on the first day, sags along with the gear. The sag wagon has a lot of advantages that are made possible by traveling in a group of twenty or so. Repair facilities and parts can be brought along where they might otherwise have to be left behind. Also, someone whose three o'clock blister ought to be pampered can pamper it and not miss the rest of the ride.

The advantages of traveling in a group are all here, and the disadvantage of regimented riding is minimized. Your only commitment is to reach the overnight stop at the end of the day. Lodging is always at an inn or motel, not a luxurious one certainly, but one that costs from four to seven dollars a night. In tune with the civilized and casual spirit of these rides, you can join and leave a tour where you will so long as you arrange to do so ahead of time.

Aside from the tours, your membership dues get

you three or four standard mailings during the year, a schedule of tours, and a membership list. You can also write for free bulletins that are pretty good little guides outlining some of the things a tourist should think about:

> What to take and how to pack
> Bicycle touring in the U.S.
> Bicycle touring in Europe
> Itineraries for cycling in Europe
> Custom-built touring bicycles

The IBTS is open to any adult (i.e., person over the age of twenty-one) who has a bike and wants to ride. Dues are $3.00 for a calendar year and have to be supplemented with about $5.00 for the expenses of scouting a tour. Huff-and-Puffers vary in age from twenty-four to seventy-two with the majority between thirty and sixty.

Write to Doctor Graves and The International Bicycle Touring Society if you'd like to join or want more information:

> 846 Prospect Street
> La Jolla, California   92037

The League of American Wheelmen

The League of American Wheelmen was founded in 1880 by a group of cyclists impressed with the work of the English organized Cyclist's Touring Club. By 1898 the American league membership had grown to over one hundred thousand. The league's influence was a significant factor in the opening of roads to bicycles in the days when the things were new to the U.S. The LAW operated a touring service that supplied maps, itineraries, and information vital to anyone traveling by bicycle in the 1890s. In its heyday the LAW was the center of horseless travel.

The automobile killed the league. By 1902, only four years after the peak of its membership, dues payers numbered only about 8,500. With time, the LAW's ranks dwindled even further.

The LAW was revived in the 1960s by a few dedicated cyclists and the help of some, but very few, financially interested parties. Today it is a growing association that again has an interest in opening roads and organizing bikeways for cyclists. It is an active national lobby, working its own peculiar and limited revenge on the horseless carriage. Oddly, the difficulties of the bicyclist haven't changed and so the goals of the LAW remain very similar to those held in the 1880s. Right-of-way is still a problem, access to roads is still limited, the automobile is even more a threat to bicycling safety, and what's left of the railroads doesn't take kindly to the bicycle.

As an organization the League of American Wheelmen promotes bicycling in general and makes significant efforts to educate riders not only in technique and safety, but also, in those things that will affect the rider, like legislation.

Aside from these activities and their obvious relation to touring, the LAW distributes a nationwide roster of its members and officers. Almost all members will be glad to help you in obtaining information about local conditions. This makes it possible for you to plan a trip before you leave on it and know pretty well what conditions you are likely to encounter. Questions about weather and roads can in this way be answered so that you don't end up pedaling into the wind over a freshly tarred road.

The LAW will also help you with individual inquiries about your machine and bicycling problems in your area. If you'd like to start a bikeway the LAW and Bicycle Institute of America are two organizations that can help you get started and put you in touch with others in your community who may help. They've got 'how-to' sheets outlining what to do.

The league is an organization that is interested regardless of what aspect of the sport you are involved in. Their goals are general enough to encompass just about anything you and your wheels want to do. Their experience and resources are growing and you can have some influence yourself on what happens to bicycling by getting in touch with both them and the Bicycle Institute of America.

League of American Wheelmen
5118 Foster Avenue
Chicago, Illinois   60630

The Bicycle Institute of America

The Bicycle Institute of America is a bicycling trade association. It seems their efforts on behalf of the industry were defined rather early and remains a general promotion of the sport rather than the equipment sold by the firms they represent.

The BIA distributes articles, pamphlets, and small books on a wide variety of subjects relating to bicycling. Their main interest is developing good facilities and safe riders. In order to do so they make an excellent library available. All you need do is send for the stuff:

1) A catalogue of bicycle movies
2) *Bicycle Riding Clubs*
3) *Bike Racing on the Campus*
4) *Bike Regulations in the Community*
5) *Bike Fun*
6) *Bicycle Safety*
7) *Bikeways*
8) *Boom in Bikeways* (a free monthly publication)

The BIA is also a clearing house for all kinds of information. For instance they have a bunch of plans for car-top bike carriers and all the pamphlets I know of that are published by municipalities and states on their own bikeways. This last storehouse could be a real boon to the cyclist on his way somewhere. The BIA Directory is reviewed with books and magazines and is certainly helpful to any cyclist.

Any promotional organization ends up a lobby of some kind, and the BIA, like the LAW, is doing a good job of organizing the fast growing interest in the sport. Again, you can help by writing them:

> Bicycle Institute of America, Inc.
> 122 East 42nd Street
> New York, New York   10017

Bicycle Touring Information

Clifford L. Franz is a talkative guy whom I happen to like very much. We've never met, but the fact that he'll help anybody doing anything involving bicycles and spends a lot of time and money doing just that has endeared him to this fledgling publisher. He is the Northern California director of the League of American Wheelmen.

Mr. Franz's service is a simple one. He offers excellent touring information at cost in exchange for your favorite, local bicycle tour (mapped). You send your data, he sends you:

1) Recommended routes on detailed section or state maps
2) A list of campgrounds or motels or both along the route
3) Check lists on what to take along for men and women

4) A guide for camping from the bike
5) For added protection, a list of the names and addresses of League of American Wheelmen officers along the route so that you can call upon them for up-to-the-minute information about roads and conditions

Mr. Franz specializes in cross-country routes and California and Pacific Coast tours. But he can also be of help concerning any part of the U.S. or Canada and would appreciate hearing from you concerning your ride.

Clifford L. Franz
36 Grand Boulevard
San Mateo, California   94401

The British Cycling Federation

The British Cycling Federation not only governs racing in Britain but also has a large and active touring section that can be very helpful to the tourist headed abroad. Their handbook is the best anywhere and like the Bicycle Institute of America's 'Bicycle Clubs Directory' it is one of the original 'access to information' catalogues. Even if you're completely ignorant of Europe and the bicycling facilities there, this little marvel of a book will guide you through unscathed.

Americans can and often do join the BCF in order to take advantage of their other fine services. In addition to touring advice their benefits include free legal aid (win, lose, or draw), third party insurance, and subscriptions to a good publication.

Simply inquiring at their offices by mail will yield you a pile of really well organized and clearly presented advice. They provide addresses for further information which will exhaust and instincts toward planning your trip thoroughly and which are proven sources of good information.

If you're cycling abroad be sure to contact them:

> British Cycling Federation
> 26 Park Crescent
> London, England

You should also write to the Cyclist's Touring Club, an English club that is very active and helpful:

> Cyclist's Touring Club
> 69 Meadow
> Godalming, Surrey
> England

BICYCLE CARRIERS

by Phillip Gregg

American cities and towns have begun working out commuter routes for bicycles. Bikeways and park openings are just a few of the improvements that cyclists all over the country are managing to get accepted by local governments. But, regardless of the facilities that are made available to cyclists in the city, you still have to pedal in the city to enjoy them. Getting out is a problem if you only have a weekend, and it's made even worse by the fact that most modern mega-sprawls can be escaped only on roads that are restricted to automobiles.

As much as you may criticize cars, you may finally have to load your bike on one in order to get to where you want to be before you start your tour. The size of cities and the traffic on their roads demands it. But you can't get two bikes in a car, so you've got to fasten them to the outside of it. As many as four machines can be loaded on top of even a compact and two or three can be added to the back. The racks that make this possible are cheap and easy to use, so you can tie your bike on and go. It's easy.

Of the two basic kinds of car carriers, the rear end type is the simplest to load. You don't have to lift the bike six feet nor turn it upside down and secure it. You just lift a bit, hang it on the rack and strap it there.

The best known rear rack is the 'Bike Toter.' Like most rear-end racks, it consists of a couple of vertical posts with hangers and will attach easily to almost any car bumper. Attaching the rack to your car is very simple, so it doesn't have to stay there all the time and you can install it with only a big pair of pliers.

W. J. Titley invented the thing in 1961 and he's done well with it since, probably because very little innovating went into this simple, effective design and so it holds up well. Nice touches include a zinc plate finish and rubber covered hangers so that you won't beat hell out of the paint on the bike. Sadly, it's a California firm with only the beginnings of a national distribution. So unless you're a Californian, you'll probably have to mail order it:

The Bicycle Exchange
3 Bow Street
Cambridge, Massachusetts 02138

Gran Sport Cyclery
1015 West Ninth Street
Lawrence, Kansas 66044

Bike Toter, Inc.
Box 888
Santa Monica, California   90406

The cost is $15.95 postpaid.

A couple of other manufacturers include,

Gerard Metal Craftsmen, Inc.
151 West Rosecrans
Gardena, California   90247

JC-1 Industries
904 Nogales Street
Industry California   91744

And a mail order house with good looking racks:
Wheel Goods
2737 Hennepin Avenue
Minneapolis, Minnesota   55408

JC-1 Industries makes one for about $15.00 that is comparable to Bike Toter's, but is chrome and they sell it for about $20.00. It is vinyl covered. One thing about JC-1 is that if you've got what's known in their catalogue as a difficult bumper they'll send you special equipment to accommodate it. If it turns out you have a special bumper, let me know what kind of a car it comes on.

The shortcomings of rear, bumper mounted racks are relatively few. They will take only two bikes unless you start dismantling them, which sort of defeats the convenience of the things. Another, more serious problem is that they sometimes don't hold the bike up high enough. If you've got a load and bad shocks on a bumpy road, you can peel the wheels right off the bike as your car bottoms out. Bike Toter and JC-1 both make high, well out-of-the-way systems that avoid this problem.

But jacking the rack up only lessens, it doesn't eliminate, the effect of road grease and rain. A lot of garbage gets picked up and thrown around by the back end of a car and a rear rack hangs your bike right in its path. If your engine is in the rear you can't get at it so long as the rack is there and the bikes are certainly vulnerable to any bumper thumping. The only other thing is scratching the bikes one against the other while driving over rough roads. You have to be careful about loading and tying them down so that they won't rattle against each other, because none of these racks has an effective method of separating one bike from another.

The alternative is to load your machines on top of the car, and this eleminates many of the problems involved in carrying a bike behind you. More important, you can get four of them up there.

About as nifty a roof top carrier as I've seen is made by JC-1. It has all sorts of fittings so that it will hold and lock four bikes on the top of your car. It's all zinc plated and has the preferable gutter clamp attachment method rather than those unreliable suction cups for $29.95.

You can adapt any luggage rack designed for the top of a car so that it will carry bicycles. Taking steps

to protect the bike against thieves and falling off are the basic directions in which you should head. If you're using an ordinary top luggage rack be sure that, upside down, the seat and handle bars rest squarely on the two cross stays. Lash the handle bars especially well as it is they that keep the bike from tipping over. Tying the seat keeps it from wobbling off.

Whether your bike is on top or behind the car you should strap it on and then guy it securely. Old belts or toe straps are easy to use but it's safer to try some rigid elastic, like inner tubes or bungee cords stretched taut. Any purely mechanical clamp that you can adapt to holding the bike firmly in place is of course even better than tying it: try wing nuts and U bolts on the handle bars.

If you want to put three or four bicycles on top of the car alternate their directions. The bars are wider than the seat so that alternating them will give you more room and so more bikes up there.

Before driving into the garage, take the bikes off the roof.

Making your own top rack is rather simple. You can either buy a basic luggage rack from an auto supply store and adapt it, or you can start from scratch. L. L. Bean of Freeport, Maine, 04032, sells a top carrier that can be easily adapted to handle bikes. It has sixty inch crossbars and costs $25.80 postpaid. A larger size with seventy-eight inch bars will accommodate five bikes and costs $28.00 postpaid. Almost all auto supply shops carry something like these racks and many of them can be had for about $15.00.

Starting from scratch isn't as difficult as it may at first seem. The best thing about it is that you'll end up with a rack that fits the bicycles that are going to go on it and that's neither too narrow nor too wide for your car. You can also add touches like the ⅜″ foam padding specified in the racks we've reproduced here.

The only unusual pieces of equipment you'll need to make these racks are the gutter clamps that secure the rack to the car. L. L. Bean sells them. They are very strong and will easily string a 2″ x 4″ board across the top of your car. Four brackets cost $13.45 postpaid. If it's faster, you can get these 'Quick-N-Easy' roof brackets from the manufacturer: Quik-N-Easy Products, Monrovia, California 91016. Sears also sells brackets. Their catalogue number is 28G-7216L if you want to order them.

The plans you'll find here are some of those available. These come from Charles 'Chick' Mead of Marion, Massachusetts, and are extremely versatile, not only for carrying bikes but also anything else you may want to throw on top of your car. Two basic sizes are given here, and by figuring from the center line of the rack you can make changes to suit your car. If you want to shop around, you can get more free 'Do-It-Yourself' plans from:

The Bicycle Institute of America
122 East 42nd Street
New York, New York   10017

"Chick" Mead's 4-Bicycle Peg Rack

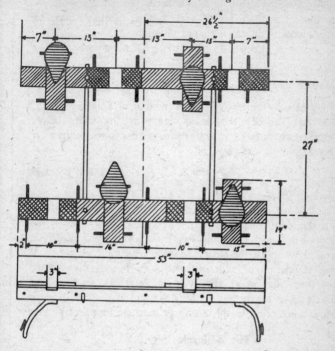

Materials needed for the 4-Bicycle Peg Rack.

1 set (4 brackets) Sears' Best Catalogue #28G-7216L.

2 pieces of 2″ x 4″ wood for racks 53″ long. Select lumber that is smooth and without knots and 9′ long if available.

1 quart of 'Penta-Treet' or some other wood preservative.

12 carriage bolts ¼″ by 1⅝″ long. Countersink the heads of these bolts ³⁄₁₆″ into the wood. (Four of these are to be used attaching the side struts to the cross pieces and eight of them attaching the brackets to the rack.)

64 large rubber bands for all pegs of the whole carrier.

4 tubes (or bulk) of weatherstrip adhesive to stick on the padding.

1 pint of 'Rustoleum' paint.

1 quart of liquid 'Neoprene' for waterproofing the top of the padding if necessary.

The diagram of the 4-bicycle carrier shows two relatively small, unshaded struts running between the two cross pieces. As illustrated, these are 2″ x 3″ lumber mortised into the cross pieces. You can also use aluminum:

2 pieces ⅛″ thick x 1″ x 32″ long flat aluminum.

If you'd like to make the cross pieces adjustable, instead of flat stock, use ¾″ angle stock.

Chick Mead's carriers call for a number of aluminum pegs. You can simplify the design somewhat by using heavy eyebolts or screws. Attach them in the same places. If you're going to use pegs, get:

12 feet of ⅜″ or ⁷⁄₁₆″ aluminum roundstock for 16 pegs 9″ long.

Chick Mead also suggests mill ends, thick felt, or carpeting for the roof rack's protective padding. Try to get the 'indoor-outdoor' carpeting, as it won't mildew and you won't have to use the Neoprene waterproofing listed above. If you decide on a foam of some sort, be sure it's closed cell foam that won't absorb water. You can get 'Ensolite' foams from nearly any mountaineering shop. (See Eastern Mountain Sports in the listing of outdoor suppliers.)

The 5-Bicycle Peg Rack

This rack is made very similarly, but you'll simply have to add some pegs and screws to the mix. Of course, where the 4-bicycle rack employs aluminum or 2″ x 3″ connecting struts, the 5-bicycle rack uses an all 2″ x 4″ design. As with the 2″ x 3″ in the 4-bicycle rack, you'll have to mortise in these struts.

Of course, there's more lumber.

2 pieces of 2″ x 4″ lumber, 60 inches long.
5 pieces of 2″ x 4″ lumber, 40 inches long.
And there are 30 instead of 16 pegs.

The bottom of each diagram shows a rear view of the rack and illustrates how the padding is added and the struts mortised into the cross pieces. Note, on the 4-bicycle rack, that there is a 3″ channel cut to allow the handlebar stem and cables to be mounted without difficulty. Extra padding

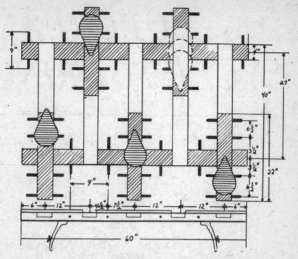

is added to further protect these bicycle parts. On the 5-bicycle rack, the simpler system is illustrated. On this rack you can simply mortise the 2″ x 4″ struts more deeply into the cross bars than is shown and add padding as on the 4-bicycle rack.

Suggestions

To make those large rubber bands mentioned, get some old motorcycle, auto, or light truck inner tubes, or buy some new ones if you'd like, and cut bands approximately one inch or more in width. Figure on four or five rubber bands for each nine inch peg. Motorcycle inner tubes are excellent.

If you want the rack to be visible at night, reflectorize it using 3M's 'Scotchlite' white or yellow 'Codit' aerosol spray cans or brush on 'reflective' paint. You can use white or yellow tape made by 3M on the metal parts to make your carrier even more visible.

Mounting bicycles: Start with the seat first. Put one rubber band over it to hold it in place. Next, put one band over each side of the handlebars and add, as needed, more, to insure against the unlikely possibility of one breaking.

EUROPEAN CYCLE TOURING

by Peter Knottley

The author, Peter Knottley, and his bicycle loaded with gear. Photograph by the British Cycling Bureau.

I once returned to England from New York on a charter liner carrying 1,100 Americans and 3 Europeans, of whom I was one. The Americans were all young, members of groups sponsored by various organizations, making their first trip to Europe. Naturally, they had little idea what to expect, and I shall always remember the universal surprise which they exhibited when we sailed up the English Channel and the cliffs and green fields of England came into view.

Knowing that Britain is a small place with a large population, everyone thought that there could not possibly be any open country left! They had imagined a small island—or rather a group of small islands—with towns so close together as to present an almost uninterrupted suburbia; they felt too that other European countries must sometimes be like that.

It isn't true, as the passengers on the ship were all soon to discover; especially those who were members of the American Youth Hostels group whom I was to take cycling in Europe for eight weeks. We in Britain have our big cities and unsightly development, but there remains a vast amount of open country of tremendous variety for so small a land—lakes, hills, pastoral, coastline, pretty villages, valleys, and the rest—and the best way to see it and to appreciate it to the full is to cycle through it.

Cycling is perhaps the *only* way to savour the pleasures of touring completely. The cyclist is utterly independent, travels fast enough to get places yet slow enough to see them and to meet the people in them and is the only traveller who can claim to be really carefree.

The same is true of other European countries. All have their centers of industry and sprawling residential areas but also have their open countryside which offers a wide variety of scenes: everything from the intimate

55

beauty of Britain to the wild, mountainous regions of the Alps and Pyrenees.

Another respect in which my American friends were agreeably surprised was that they found that we Europeans do enjoy a higher material standard of living than they had expected. With a few exceptions, you do find electric shaver outlets in our hotels and hostels, television everywhere, and all the other trappings of what we are pleased to call civilization! So you do not need to bring with you anything except personal necessities; I hope and believe that, although national tastes and habits inevitably vary (which is part of the joy of touring), you will find that we are able and very willing to cater for your every need when you come to visit us.

You will find that cyclists are especially respected and welcomed everywhere, a pleasant fact that I have never been able to explain and can only attribute to the natural sympathy and interest which the genuinely active and himself sympathetically curious traveler arouses.

Here are some notes about cycle touring in Europe I hope will prove helpful in allaying some doubts and providing some information.

Accommodations are under heavy pressure in the popular parts of the Continent in summer, especially in the period from mid-July to the end of August when the majority of Europeans take their annual vacations. The pressure is equally great on hotels of every grade, guest houses, and youth hostels, so that if you plan to use the popular routes of resorts as overnight stops, bookings should be made in advance.

But the cycle tourist does not take kindly to planning where he must be every night, so it is helpful to know that away from the haunts of the masses who seek sophisticated amusements—and usually only a very short distance away—accommodations may be had at short notice—even on only a few hours notice.

This means that provided you are willing to stay overnight in the countryside, which is more agreeable, quiet, and cheap than in town, you may look for your room for the night during the afternoon of that very day. Since this applies as mentioned even within a few miles of popular resorts, you are within reach of the sophisticated amusements should you want them.

Every country has a tourist department which publishes annually a comprehensive list of accommodations of all grades, with the facilities and price of every establishment given. You can get this information from the tourist office of the countries concerned in most major cities abroad.

With the exception of a few eastern European countries, all countries on the Continent now have a chain of youth hostels. These offer simple, inexpensive dormitory accommodations, and the European section of the International Youth Hostel handbook lists the locations of the majority of hostels in Europe with brief details of their size and the facilities they offer. The handbook may be obtained from the headquarters of American Youth Hostels Inc. at 20 West 17th St., New York, N.Y., 10011. AYH also arranges a number of fine group cycling tours to Europe, under expert leaders.

Each individual country also publishes annually its own handbook of hostels (in its own language) which gives much more detail and includes even the smallest and most remote of the hostels.

To be completely independent and to feel free to

roam and stop at will, an increasing number of cyclists are turning to cycle camping. If 'camping' conveys to you the thought of the immense amount of equipment conveyed by the motorist, making the thought of cycle camping seem quite heroic, it must be stated that a skillful cycle camper will be able to stow all his needs, including tent and cooking equipment, into a saddle bag and panniers with ease.

Tents are available for two to four people which weigh—complete with pegs, ground sheet and fly-sheet —between 3½ and 6 pounds, and lightweight sleeping bags weigh about 2½ to 3 pounds. They pack into very small bags. The more in the cycling party, the more there are to share the load and camping becomes no more of a problem luggagewise than any other method of cycle touring.

Most European countries are well provided with official camping sites (some of them also very crowded in summer) and lists of these are available from the national tourist offices. But the glory of camping is the possibility it offers of pitching for the night in good natural sites away from the holiday crowds.

When planning a tour in Europe, remember that particular areas may conveniently be linked by train journeys if time does not allow for cycling all the way. In all European countries except Britain, carriage of a cycle by train is very cheap, even over long distances. In Britain is costs half the second-class passenger fare, which is greatly in excess of the charge in any other country. Note also that in some countries (where the facility is most appreciated, e.g., Norway) buses may also be used for the transportation of cycles.

Generally speaking, there are no special visa or vaccination requirements in the countries of Europe, but you should check every time whether the U.S. government requires inoculation against any illness before your

reentry after visiting any foreign country. Similarly, visa requirements should be checked as the various national regulations do change from time to time.

Concern is sometimes expressed that water supplies may be impure and unfit to drink abroad. This worry is unfounded; if a public fountain or other water source is unfit to drink, it will display a notice to that effect. All over Europe, villages retain their street water pumps and fountains and there need be no fear of using them.

If you have any reservations about any water source, then, unless a known pure supply can be found, the water should be boiled before use. Water purifying tablets are obtainable and to carry a small supply is no hardship. But the problem is unlikely to arise in western Europe.

Road regulations applicable to cyclists vary a little between countries but are not onerous. In some countries it is obligatory to use cycle paths where they exist (but not in others; Britain, for example does not impose the obligation). Again, in some countries (not in Britain), it is necessary to ride in single file. These variations in regulations are not so great as to warrant action before the tour; they are quickly discovered upon arrival in each country. Road signs and instructions are rapidly becoming standardized all over Europe and their meanings are quite clear. For night riding, you need a white front lamp, red rear lamp, and red rear reflector.

Mosquitoes and midges are a nuisance sometimes, and many people will need to use some preparation to

59

keep them at bay. They are especially troublesome near lakes and rivers and in humid climates; in July in Scotland, for example, they are often extremely irritating. In southern Europe, too, they can be a nuisance. The cyclist has an advantage here because the sheer motion of riding prevents insects settling on the person very often; but as soon as you halt the problem is with you.

Your bank will provide you with current rates of exchange of European currencies. Note those applicable to the countries you intend to visit. In most countries in Europe you will find the cost of living appreciably cheaper than at home; Switzerland, Belgium, France and Germany are relatively expensive and other Common Market countries are finding that food prices are rapidly rising, but Spain is particularly economical to visit.

It is regretted that it is necessary to advise you to be sure that you pay the right prices for goods and services, and no more, when on tour in Europe. In an endeavour to suppress the unfortunate tendency of most of those connected with the tourist industry to charge visitors too much, the various national authorities publish prices of hotel rooms, fares, and other public services, and these must be publicly displayed. It is thus not too difficult to confirm the price charged. Shops usually display their prices, as do restaurants; if they do not, avoid them. Service charges where authorized are also displayed (for example, scales of porters' fees at railway stations) or these charges are included at a fixed percentage in the bill (for example, in restaurants). No other tipping is necessary, unless you feel that a particularly acceptable degree of assistance has been given and you wish to show appreciation.

What follows are some notes I think relevant to some of the best touring areas in the world. If this is to be your first time abroad you will want to supplement these sketches with more information. These, I hope, offer information that is especially significant to the bicyclist and that I find important when touring in these countries.

THE BRITISH ISLES

Here, at least, you will not have any major language problems! But you will find diverse dialects in every small district and one or two of them (for example, in the northeast of England and in Wales) may give a little difficulty at first.

The British Isles comprise the two principal islands of Great Britain and Ireland and numerous small islands which either stand alone or in groups. The tremendous diversity of landscape, with dramatic changes of scenery within quite small areas, is due to the fact that almost every stage of the geological succession is contained within these islands.

All this makes the country one of the most interesting for cycling, bearing in mind the many historic cities and towns and associations of particular appeal to our cousins from across the Atlantic. Readers will have heard one fact about this country which will be borne out by experience—that we have weather and not a climate. Generally mild and humid, it can be cool in summer and warm in winter; rainfall varies between twenty and two hundred inches in different localities but is rarely continuous for twenty-four hours. One can only say that it is necessary to be prepared, even in summer, which unpredictably may produce weeks of warm sunshine or of mild wet conditions.

But Britain would not be the green and flowered land it is if it weren't wet. These characteristics are typical of the downland and moorland of the south, the plains of the east, and the uplands of Wales and the north. Only in a few regions of England, some of the northern isles and the more remote areas of Scotland are there rugged, bare mountains and rocky outcrops.

In common with much of Europe, motor traffic is heavy in Britain, but some 80% of it uses only about 15% of the road mileage—the freeways and other major routes. There is an unequalled network of good roads carrying little, and sometimes almost no, traffic. This allows easy access to the best of the countryside and villages and makes cycling a real pleasure. But in the summer, the high spots such as London, Stratford-upon-Avon, Oxford, Edinburgh, and many other places are congested with tourists. It is better to find accommodations a few miles away from such spots and to visit them on day trips.

Scotland is thinly populated outside the cities and is more mountainous than the rest of the British Isles. The mountains are not high by general standards; there are over five hundred peaks rising to more than 3,000 ft., but the highest is only 4,406 ft. (Ben Nevis, the highest in the British Isles.) Yet their grandeur is out of all proportion to their heights.

The Welsh mountains have a special appeal to British cyclists, being less high, yet similarly grand, and giving the possibility of cycling routes using green tracks as well as surfaced roads. These are completely safe and rideable. Ireland is a popular touring country too; there, traffic is much lighter and the extreme natural hospitality of the Irish ensures you'll learn more about the place than what it looks like. In both Wales and Ireland, there are still some areas where the national languages are spoken, but it is extremely uncommon to find anyone who does not speak English.

NORWAY

Norway is a rocky country, noted for its coastline of many fjords, inlets and bays surrounded by mountains. These indentations give the coast a total length of an astounding 21,000 miles of magnificent scenery and the western fjords, with a climate similar to that of Britain, form the most interesting area for cycle touring.

The great fjords penetrate miles into the mountains, becoming narrower towards the head while the enclosing mountains become higher and steeper. Thus, road distances are deceptive because they wind around the fjords. These roads sometimes have steep pitches and are often roughly paved or are simply unimproved dirt and rock. Nevertheless, the extreme beauty of the country and, in spring, the masses of flowers, make it well worthwhile to visit.

A tour should be well planned. When you're mapping out your ride you should note that cycles are usually carried by local buses in Norway. There is a good, but complex, coastal steamer service between the coast towns which is also useful to know about when planning. A steamer journey is a pleasant interlude, enables the coastline to be seen from another vantage point, and can make a useful link in the chain of a tour.

To the east, five great valleys run north and west from Oslo fjord, and the broad rivers penetrate the forests to open moorland and wide valleys. Each valley has its particular way of life, architecture and scenic attractions.

The south coast of Norway is unlike the rest of the country. It has no fjords, enjoys tree-covered hills which are less steep and high and has many bathing beaches and holiday resorts. At the other end of the country and of the scale, travel continues over unpaved roads and snow-covered mountains to well within the Arctic Circle

—'the land of the midnight sun'. This is visible at Bodo from June 1 to July 13, at Tromso from May 18 to July 25, and at the North Cape from May 12 to August 1.

Cyclists regularly reach the far north of Norway. Thanks to the Gulf Stream and the long hours of sunshine, the weather is mild and the lowlands are neither wild nor barren.

English is widely spoken in Norway.

SWEDEN

Spring is the best time to see Sweden. In a few weeks in May the winter snows thaw and the sun rapidly increases its intensity, becoming really bright for the short summer which lasts only until August. During this time the hours of sunshine exceed those of Italy and Spain, although the temperature rarely goes above 70° F. What rainfall there is consists of short, sharp showers.

Over half the country is covered with somber forests, yet a wide variety of flora gives a show of color everywhere you go.

Sweden is a large country with many different landscapes, and it would take many weeks to explore the land fully by cycle. As in the case of many countries, an exploration of one or two areas will normally have to suffice. It must be remembered that even though the cyclist cannot see every place, he at least makes a close acquaintance with a few. Finally, the bicyclist will visit places that the faster traveler will miss entirely even though he has passed through them.

Arriving at Gothenburg or Stockholm, the area of canals and lakes of central Sweden are within reach. To the west of the lakes lie Bohuslän (fishing villages and resorts) and Dalsland (small farms and lakes). The province of Dalarna is fine for touring because local dress and customs survive here and the surroundings of woods, mountains, small churches, and farms are very interesting.

Skäne is good agricultural country with parks and gardens of old castles and houses. Farther north there are more forests, lakes, and mountains; a railway line from Stockholm makes a convenient approach to this area.

DENMARK

Denmark consists of the peninsula of Jutland, projecting north from Germany, and some five hundred other islands (four hundred uninhabited) of which two, Zealand and Funen, are the most important. The whole country is but half the size of Scotland, and is primarily agricultural.

Pleasant rolling downland with no hills of note joins small towns and villages of charm and historic interest. July is the best month for warm weather—average 60° F. Later on in the summer there is appreciable rainfall.

Quiet and homely, with friendly folk, Denmark is a very pleasant place to cycle.

WEST GERMANY

In general, this large central European country consists of three belts—the narrow strip of the Alps, which lie within its southern borders, the central uplands, and the northern lowlands. The climate is less capricious than in the coastal countries, being cold in winter, hot in summer. There are many dialects of the German language, but English is quite widely understood in the larger towns.

Unless you are an experienced cyclist, don't take a machine with narrow lightweight wheels and tires to Germany, where there are sometimes poor road surfaces and more important, where there are frequently long stretches of cobbled roads and tram tracks.

The road system is, however, very good and all

parts of Germany have access by rideable lanes and minor roads. There are a large number of interesting areas, too numerous to describe in detail; in any European tour some part of the country will certainly fall naturally on the route and specific information should be sought accordingly.

THE NETHERLANDS

Americans and British say 'Holland,' but Holland is only one province of the kingdom properly called the Netherlands.

A very flat and highly developed country—one fifth is below sea level, protected by dykes from the ocean—Holland is a small kingdom where you'll feel a member of the family as soon as you arrive. Heavily populated, Holland remains a land of bicycles, and special cycle paths exist through woods and parks. Some of the paths are forbidden to motorists.

Lack of protecting hills makes cycling westward, against the prevailing wind, quite tiring. A tour from Amsterdam, around the Ijesselmeer and then back to Amsterdam would be about five hundred miles in length and then take in most of the country. You should allow fourteen days for this route. An alternative crossing of the land in a few days as part of a longer tour of several countries would enable much of the clean, pleasant and historic Netherlands to be appreciated. English is widely spoken.

BELGIUM

Also a small kingdom, south of the Netherlands, Belgium is second only to it in density of population. The people form two groups; in the north and west the Flemings, speaking a language almost the same as Dutch, and in the south the Walloons, who speak French and their own dialects of French. Belgium has much agriculture, mining, and heavy industry, and although the whole country is of interest historically, the only really attractive scenery is in the Ardennes hills at the southeast corner. These rise to two thousand feet and are rolling, wooded, unspoiled hills that are ideal for cycling.

LUXEMBOURG

A tiny country, just fifty miles by thirty-five, Luxembourg has very attractive scenery and many historic associations. The northern part is a continuation of the Ardennes hills with altitudes of about two thousand feet. The rest of the country is known as Gutland and is also hilly. The hills here, however, go only as high as five hundred feet—a continuation of the hills of the Lorraine. All the roads are good, all are hilly (fairly steep but not long hills) and the entire country is very attractive.

FRANCE

"Everyone has two countries—his own and France." This saying sums up the general appeal of France, which has the greatest variety of landscapes of any European country. An infinite number of regional characteristics, people, food and geographical features, coupled with an influence which for two thousand years has benefited the arts, make France a study in itself.

For the cyclist, France has a network of good roads giving access to all parts; cobbles remain here and there in towns, but otherwise surfaces are good and signposting excellent. Cycle racing is a highly popular sport in France, and visiting cyclists of all kinds are welcome and are the objects of interest. Any help required is willingly given, and the humblest garage—in the absence of a cycle dealer—will usually deal with any mechanical problems you may have. The French Cycle Touring Federation is very active and seeks to promote international travel.

SWITZERLAND

Switzerland is a mountainous country; the Swiss Alps are the highest and finest part of the Alpine chain, and they cover over one-half of the land. The Jura mountains occupy another one-sixth of it. The highest peak is Monte Rosa, 15,217 feet.

The range of climate, because of the mountains, is very great. There are numerous passes through the mountains, which range in height from 2,500 to almost 9,000 feet. The higher ones are open only for several weeks in midsummer when the snows temporarily recede and are cold all the time. These passes are extremely popular with European cycle tourists who think nothing of setting out to conquer a dozen or so of them during their two or three weeks of annual vacation.

The climbs are long rather than very steep, and with adequately low gearing they present no difficulty and considerable satisfaction to the cyclist. Road surfaces are generally excellent.

Switzerland is a very clean and attractive country with a high standard of living.

AUSTRIA

Chains forming the eastern extension of the Alps run from west to east across Austria; although not quite so high as those in Switzerland, peaks rise to 10,000 to 12,500 feet. There are also two lake districts, the Salzkammergut and the Corinthian.

Main roads are well surfaced and engineered but secondary roads are often rough and have many twists and turns. The fine scenery makes Austria another popular cycling country, and its attraction is enhanced by the courteous ways and carefree outlook of the people.

ITALY

Northern Italy is dominated by the southern Alps which form the country's frontier with France, Switzerland, and Austria (the highest mountain in the Alps, Mont Blanc, 15,782 feet, is on the Franco-Italian border). The northern plain separates the Alps from the Apennines, a mountain range forming the 'spine' of the country. The large islands of Sardinia and Sicily and the smaller ones of Elba and Capri are also part of Italy. Within these areas there is a great diversity of peoples, industry, culture, and environment.

Summer weather is hot, increasingly so the farther south one travels; Sicily and the Gulf of Taranto can produce temperatures of almost 100°F. (higher in the sun) in July and August.

The whole country is visited regularly by cycle tourists, and Italy is similar to France in that cycling is a widely followed activity and the cyclist always arouses interest. Roads and facilities are good, but they deteriorate somewhat as one goes further south and the country becomes more thinly populated and less productive.

Italy is well endowed with treasures of art and culture. Cities like Rome, Florence, Venice, and many others warrant thorough exploration.

SPAIN

Another kaleidoscope of landscapes presents itself in Spain. The Meseta (central plateau) is crossed with mountain ranges. In the south, the plateau ends abruptly to give way to the Andalusian basin, between which and the Mediterranean coast lies the snowcapped Sierra Nevada which has the highest point in Spain, the Pico de

Mulhacen, 11,420 feet. The Catalonian coast is dramatic; the nearby Pyrenees form the frontier with France and a natural barrier between the Iberian peninsula and the rest of Europe.

The climate is again regional but is generally warm and humid. Cycling is easiest in the north and down the east coast to Barcelona where there are good roads; in central Spain heat and dusty roads make the going less easy. New tires and low gears are recommended.

PORTUGAL

Stretching back for distances of 140 miles in the north and 70 miles in the south from the southwestern seaboard of the Iberian peninsula, Portugal is cut by deep river valleys from east to west. The part of the country north of the Tagus is hilly behind the coastal plain, and apart from the scenic area around Braganca in the northeast is well cultivated and the population (though small in total) widely spread.

South of the Tagus, wild heathlands alternate with oak and olive forests and extensive wheat fields. The coast of the southernmost province, the Algarve, is similar to that of Andalusia in Spain and of North Africa and is increasingly being developed with holiday resorts. Summer in the Algarve is hot, but the rest of the country enjoys a more moderate climate.

Roads are, in general, good—better than in Spain —and, although sometimes cobbled, they are not uneven and are quite acceptable for cycling.

The foregoing is an all-too-brief sketch of the most likely west European countries to be visited by cycle tourists. Of course, much more could be written about each one; to do so would be beyond the scope of this

70

publication and in any case most tourists will want to obtain their own specific information about the places they are going to visit, according to the time at their disposal and their personal interests.

There is no reason why one should not cycle in countries not mentioned, such as Finland, Yugoslavia, Greece, the Balkan countries, Czechoslovakia, and Poland, although there are more formalities in the case of communist lands. Southeastern Europe, however, particularly Yugoslavia and Greece, are visited by numerous cycle tourists annually—those who like hot sunshine, less sophisticated conditions, and wilder countryside.

There are few places where one can go and not go by bicycle, so if your own fancy has not been mentioned, it doesn't mean it isn't possible!

FOREIGN FEDERATIONS

The following is a list of Federations affiliated to the Union Cycliste Internationale. Many operate touring services and may be able to help you with detailed information if you call at their offices or write to them.

ALBANIA Federata Sportive Shaiptare-Bruga, Abdi Toptani, 3, Tirana.

ARGENTINA Federacion Ciclista Argentina, Av. Pte. Figueroa, Alcorta 4600, Buenos Aires.

AUSTRALIA (Amateur) Amateur Cyclists' Association of Australia, W. S. Young, 34 Wardell Road, Earlswood, Sydney, New South Wales.

AUSTRALIA (Professional) Australian Federal Cycling Council, S. R. Freshwater, 47 Westminster Street, Bexley, New South Wales.

71

AUSTRIA Österreischiche Radsport Kommission, Prinz Eugenstrasse 12, Vienna IV.

BELGIUM Ligue Velocipedique Belge, 8 Place des Martyrs, Brussels.

BRAZIL Brazilian Confederation of Sports, Rua da Quittanda 3, 2nd Andar, Case Postale 1078, Rio-de-Janeiro.

BULGARIA Federation Bulgare de Cyclisme, Boulevard Tolbouk hine 18, Sofia.

CANADA Canadian Cycling Association, 3737 rue Monselet, Montreal Nord, P.Q.

CHINA National Athletic Federation of China, 3 Tai Yang Kung, Peking.

CZECHOSLOVAKIA Ceskoslovenska Sekce Cyklistiky, Na Porici 12, Prague 1.

DENMARK (Amateur) Danmarks Cykle Union, Gronneraenge 21, 2920 Charlottenlund, Copenhagen.

DENMARK (Professional) Dansk Professionelt Cykle Forbund, Grambyvei 56, 2610 Rodovre.

EAST GERMANY · Deutscher Radsport Verband, Kochhannstrasse 1, 1034 Berlin.

FINLAND Suomen Pyorailyliitto, Yrjonkato 21b, Helsinki.

FRANCE Federation Francaise de Cyclisme, 1 rue Ambroise-Thomas, Paris 9e.

GREECE Hellenic Amateur Athletic Association, 4 rue Kapsali, Athens.

HOLLAND Koninklijke Nederlandsche Wielren Unie, 15 Nieuwe Uitleg, The Hague.

HUNGARY Magyar Kerekparos Szoveteg Millenaris Sporttelep, Szabo Jozsef u3, Budapest XIV.

IRISH REPUBLIC Irish Cycling Federation, 72 Prospect Avenue, Glasnevin, Dublin, 9.

ITALY   Federazione Ciclistica Italiana, Palazzo delle Federazione Viale Tiziano 70, Rome.

JAPAN   Japanese Cycling Federation, Kishi Memorial Hall, 25 Kannami-Cho-Shipuyaku, Tokyo.

LUXEMBOURG   Federation du Sport Cycliste Luxembourgeois, Case Postale 145, Luxembourg City.

MEXICO   Federacion Mexicana de Ciclismo, Confederation Sportive Mexicaine, Avenue Juarez Num 64-311, Mexico City 1.

NEW ZEALAND   New Zealand Amateur Cycling Association, C.P.O. Box 30459, Lower Hutt.

NORTHERN IRELAND   Northern Ireland Cycling Federation, S. Martin, 13 Premier Drive, Belfast 15.

NORWAY   Norges Cykleforbund, Youngstorget, 1 Oslo.

PHILIPPINES   Philippine Cycling Association, Rizal Memorial Track-Football Stadium, Dakota Street, Manila.

POLAND   Polska Zwiazek Kolarska, 1 Plac Xelaznej Bramy, Warsaw.

PORTUGAL   Federacao Potuguesa de Ciclismo, Rua Barros Queiroz 29-1, Lisbon.

RUMANIA   Federatia Romina de Ciclismo, Vasile Conta, 16, Bucarest.

RUSSIA   Federation Cycliste U.S.S.R., Skatertnyi Pereoulok 4, Moscow 69.

SPAIN   Federacion Española de Ciclismo, Alfonso XII 36, 1st Dacha, Madrid 14.

SWEDEN   Svenska Cykelforbundet, Stora Nygatan 41-43, Stockholm C.

SWITZERLAND (**German-speaking Cantons**)   Schweiz Radfahrer-u-Motofahrer-Bund, Schaffhauserstrasse 272, Zurich 57.

SWITZERLAND (**French-speaking Cantons**) Union Cycliste Suisse, 4 Rue du Vieux-College, 1211 Geneva, 3.

UNITED STATES (**Amateur**)   Amateur Bicycle League of America, 87-66, 256th Street, Floral Park, L.I., New York 11001.

UNITED STATES (**Professional**) National Cycling Association, Frank Semcer, 465 Ridgewood Road, Maplewood, New Jersey.

WEST GERMANY   Bund Deutscher Radfahrer, Westanlage 56, B.P. 263, Giessen-Lahn (Hessen.)

YUGOSLAVIA   Federation Yougoslave de Cyclisme, Hilendarska 6, Belgrade.

MAGAZINE
AND BOOK REVIEWS

MAGAZINES

Bicycling!, H. M. Leete and Company, 256 Sutter Street, San Francisco, California 94108. Monthly, twelve issues per year, $6.00.

Occupying the very favorable position of being the only bicycle magazine in the United States, Bicycling! has managed to survive with a notoriously poor record of performance and spotty editorial quality. Had there been any competition over the past years, Bicycling! would have had to improve or go under.

Most specialty magazines have at their core someone whose passion for the subject fuels the flames of editorial excellence. At Bicycling! there is no love of sport in the blood of the publisher, nor is there any cycling experience among the in-office staff. Relying on gratis contributions from cycling enthusiasts in the field, the quality varies widely from very good to very poor, with the emphasis on the latter.

In depth reporting is nonexistant. Important events are many times not even mentioned. What comes via the mailman is what gets printed, good, bad, or indifferent. On occasion it would seem Bicycling! is trying to set a record for saying less in more pages than any other publication. And the quality of the photo reproduction and subject matter is generally unacceptable.

The magazine does not take a stand on matters of concern to the sport. If the staff is aware that there are important issues at hand, they don't seem to wish to confront them.

What then, does Bicycling! have to offer? A monthly technical section by Fred DeLong presents thoroughly researched and detailed reports on all aspects of the bicycle and the physical forces involved in riding it. Occasionally there are valuable articles on maintenance and repair, road tests, and advice on how to do this or that. The question and answer section is interesting, as is the letters department.

Some very inspiring and entertaining stories of tours by clubs and individuals appear now and then, and there is always a report of a tour at home or abroad in every issue.

Through the pages of Bicycling! you will find out what and where it's happening, so at least in hindsight you can take part in next year's events when they roll around again.

What might be best about Bicycling! is what the future may hold. Three other bicycle magazines are scheduled to appear early this year. Already Bicycling! has taken the hint with promises of expanded coverage. Even with its many shortcomings it's worth the subscription price. Then you'll have twelve months to form your own opinions.

League of American Wheelmen Bulletin, 356 Robert Avenue, Wheeling, Illinois 60090. Monthly to members.

The League of American Wheelmen (LAW) is a national organization established to assist and coordinate touring activities in the United States. You must be a member to receive their bulletin, and for this reason alone membership is worth the price of the dues. The bulletin, generally twenty-four pages 8½ x 11 offset, has a homespun style which is very clubsy, but it is regular, timely, and has the most up to date and comprehensive touring calendar published anywhere. If you want to take part and really be in on the happenings, becoming a member of the league is a must.

Bicycle Clubs Directory and Other Stuff, Bicycle Institute of America, 122 East 42nd Street, New York, New York 10017. Free on request.

The bicycle clubs directory is just that, a complete listing of all the bicycle clubs in the nation, state by state, with a brief description of their activities and who to contact for further information. Also listed are national and international racing bodies, touring groups, and trade organizations. Bicycle publications, related cycling activities, a bicycle museum directory, an historical information guide, and information as to where to find bike maps, touring information, bike books, equipment, movies, bikeway advice, and much more can be yours just for the asking.

Some other magazines and periodicals that you may like to look into are listed below. Most will send you a sample copy so long as you forward the price of it and postage.

International Cycle Sport, Kennedy Brothers, Howden Hall, Howden Road, Silsden, Keighly, Yorkshire, England. Monthly, twelve issues per year, $6.00.

Le Cycliste, 18 rue de Commandeur, Paris 14, France. Monthly, twelve isssues per year, $7.00. (The text is in French.)

Cycling and Sporting Cyclists, Longacre Press, Ltd., 161-166 Fleet Street, London, England. Weekly, fifty-two weeks a year, $16.00.

Cycle Touring, the Cyclists' Touring Club, 69 Meadrow, Godalming, Surrey, England. Bimonthly, six issues per year, $2.50.

Journal of the Amateur Bicycle League of America, The Amateur Bicycle League of America, 4233 205th Street, Bayside, Long Island, New York.

Boom in Bikeways, The Bicycle Institute of America, 122 East 42nd Street, New York, New York 10017.

76

Almost all the books listed here are available from a California mail order house called Books About Bicycling. Publishers will send you the book if you send them your money, but most of them don't like to do so. Their systems are set up such that handling one piece at a time is more of an inconvenience than a profit-making service. As a result, you may have to wait quite a while before you see whatever it is you want to read.

If you order through Books About Bicycling you'll get your book at the same price and probably much faster. It is a complete book service for bicycle enthusiasts listing over twenty-five titles covering touring, racing, maintenance, history, fitness, and health. Established by Peter Hoffman, racing and touring cyclist and the former editor of American Cycling Magazine, this company helps bike riders locate books and information on the sport. They've a free catalogue; just send for it.

Books About Bicycling
Box 208t
Nevada City, California 95959

The Complete Book of Bicycling, by Eugene A. Sloane, New York, Simon and Schuster, 1970, $9.95.

Technical data in hand and years of bicycling experience available to edit and interpret that data, Mr. Sloane has written the best single volume on bicycling in print. When it comes to self propelled, two wheel travel this book touches all the bases. The only equally thorough work is in the collection reviewed below, *The Best of Bicycling!*, and that volume doesn't deal with the by now famous American heavyweights with coaster brakes and three speed hubs. Sloane covers tricycles and children as well as 'Cinellis.' Better still is the fact that Sloane writes about what's available, how to use it and how to fix it. His is a very complete book.

His illustrations are factory perfect line drawings which do nothing to humble or simplify the mechanism involved. His suggestions run in the same vein: He is an enthusiast and his appreciations have kept pace with his experience. The book, then, comes in three parts. A bicycle design appreciation course, a short history and review of present day competition, and a thorough and detailed maintenance and repair section. The business of knowing quality goods is given lots of space, though he names no names except to complement.

The book's only shortcoming is it's scope. Too much is squeezed into a small space. Of course this reviewer is involved in a large source on a small part of bicycling and so articles covering tents, for instance, can be long and studied rather than short and general. Sloane covers touring and camping in a few pages.

In fact, he covers everything, one subject at a time, in a few pages. This makes his book a great introduction to the sport. You can get here a good view, one that will allow you to understand more specific arguments and relate them to other aspects of the sport. As a technical introduction to bicycling, Sloane's book can't be beat.

Anybody's Bike Book, by Tom Cuthbertson, Berkeley, California, The Ten Speed Press, 1971, $2.95.

There is something very attractive about bicycles, something pleasing about their simple, functional appearance. Aside from all the good things inherent in riding, there is an aesthetic quality to the machines themselves that is based on their extreme simplicity and practicality. The working parts of a ten-speed are relatively few and easily gotten at for repair and maintenance. On top of that, understanding the principles of how they convert sweat into motion doesn't require a variety of graduate degrees. These two aspects of cycling makes manuals offering simple 'how-to' instructions a real possibility even for those like you and me, who are a bit clumsy and a little slow.

Tom Cuthbertson's manual is a good, healthy one. He not only knows

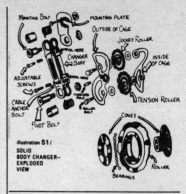

illustration 51/
SOLID
BODY CHANGER—
EXPLODED
VIEW

about fixing bikes, but also has in abundance the kind of patience that is needed in order to write a repair manual. His book is well organized and clear, to the point where he kindly indicates whether things should be turned in a clockwise direction (cl) or in a counterclockwise direction (ccl). This is the result of his stated intention: to teach people that it's not as hard as it seems and that they can take care of their bikes and fix them when they break:

"This is a book about fixing bicycles. It is written in such a way that anyone can use it to fix any bicycle. Many of you (especially the ladies) have been given the idea that if something is mechanical you can't do it. That is outrageous. Bicycles are not monstrous machines which only wizards can understand. They are all simple enough that with a little know-how and patience, anyone can work on them. *You can do it!* You don't have to know any magic. The mechanical mystique is a lie."

Another high point in Cuthbertson's book is Rick Morrall, the illustrator. His drawings are very cartoonish and simple.

anybody's bike book

an original manual of bicycle repairs

written by tom cuthbertson
illustrated by rick morrall

As a result, the exploded pictures of complicated bicycle parts are exaggerated to the point where it is possible to see the difference between one little washer and another so that you can put whatever it is you've taken apart back together. Though it's not the way to do it, you might be able to understand most of what needs fixing on a bike before ever having seen one by studying the drawings and reading the text of *Anybody's Bike Book*.

This book doesn't give repair breakdowns according to manufacturer indicating how to deal with the idiosyncracies of a particular design. So, though Cuthbertson's straightforward text helps to explain the basic principles behind repair, some of the fine points of adjustment are harder to understand.

There's one other thing: Unlike Sloane's book, Cuthbertson's isn't encyclopedic. It's a repair manual with occasional references to different bicycle designs only as they seem interesting or pertinent to repair. You'll not discover here, at least not directly nor in great depth, what to look for when you're buying.

Finally, this is a good book. It isn't thick and super-thorough and occasionally you'll have to scratch your head in an effort to fix something the first time. But, most repair guides are for people who have already repaired bicycles before and so don't have to learn what to do. *Anybody's Bike Book* is actually for the beginner, and that in itself is unusual. You can buy one at the shop where you buy your first bike and it will introduce you to the thing.

North American Bicycle Atlas, by Asa Warren, American Youth Hostels. Inc. 1970, $2.25.

Sitting with maps studying the felt marker wish plans traced on each is a necessary pretrip exercise. To the bicyclist, the problem is that maps are flat and roads often aren't, and so there is very little accurate planning possible when you haven't yet been where you're going. Well, Mr. Warren's maps have the advantage of experience and as a result they measure the distances between things that have nothing to do with miles.

Asa Warren is the western regional director for American Youth Hostels and has been involved in bicycle touring since 1949. His continuing effort to encourage both bicycling and hosteling in the U.S. on the scale that they both now enjoy in Europe has led him to compile these detailed pages.

This is an 'atlas' of bicycle tours throughout forty-seven states, six Canadian provinces, Mexico, and the Caribbean. It has ninety tours ranging in length from a week to a month with maps and texts on places of interest along the way. There are also sixty-two one-day and weekend rides mapped out.

The greatest strength of the atlas is its grading of each tour's difficulty so that you can gauge your prospects for actually doing what you plan to do in the time you plan to do it. The easiest tours cover level, improved roads for as few as nine mile jaunts. The hardest are rough, long rides with century or nearly century tours turned in daily over hilly ground and dirt roads.

Any system of gradation is bound to be criticized, and there has been some here of Mr. Warren's discussions of different tours. Generally, however, they are helpful and accurate and the routing of cyclists through the maze of American roads is very good.

Bike-Ways (101 Things to Do With a Bike), by Lillian and Godfrey Frankel, New York, Sterling Publishing Company, 1971, $2.95.

Bike-Ways is probably the most comprehensive, and therefore the most generalized, introduction to bicycle riding and related activities available. Unfortunately in attempting to cover every aspect of the sport the explanations are far too brief, many times nearly trite. Two areas of importance that need expanding are how to select and fit your bicycle, and how to ride it properly. If the novice gets off on the wrong foot in this area, the rest of the text will do him little good.

The authors, well intended judging from their emphasis on having fun with your bike, seem to have drawn on every available manufacturer's manual rather than relying on first hand knowledge, such is their style. *Bike-Ways* is by no means a literary milestone, but then few bicycle books are.

The book's greatest emphasis is on touring, bike camping, and a wide variety of games and activities for grade school age children. If you are a beginning cyclist, the advice in the first two categories will be initially useful, especially if you are a novice to camping as well. Many good points are offered for your early trips, but after your first few outings the value of the book diminishes rapidly. The fun and games outlined for the younger set are rather useless if you think of yourself as an adult cyclist, but would prove valuable when working with kids in a service club, scouting, or recreational department situation.

The advice is fundamental throughout, so if you are already in the saddle you will probably want to skip this one. As a basic guide for the newcomer to cycling, *Bike-Ways* will help break the ice and wet the appetite for more sophisticated information.

The Best of Bicycling! H. M. Leete, New York, Trident Press, 1970, available from Books About Bicycling, $9.95.

Nowhere will you find a more colorful, exciting, and informative synopsis of what cycling is all about than by reading *The Best of Bicycling!*, an anthology of articles which appeared in *American Cycling Magazine*, later *Bicycling!*, over a span of six years. This collection of the experiences and knowledge of the countries' foremost cyclists makes fascinating reading for the novice, and is an indispensible reference for the enthusiast.

Relive the frightening tale of Delva Murphy, the young Irish lass who, alone, cycled around the world, fighting for her life and her virtue every mile of the way. Read how a U. S. Army doctor saved his life by escaping from the Germans during the Battle of the Bulge on his trusty touring machine. Groove with a Jewish longhair who discovers much more than just the countryside in his perceptive "God is Alive and Well on the Prairie." Tour the backroads of France, England, Japan, Holland, Maui, California, Ohio, Vermont, Texas, or cycle the mountain trails with the 'Phantom of the Rockies.'

The Best of **Bicycling!**

Edited by Harley M. Leete

Seventy-nine lively and informative articles from America's most popular cycling magazine

Thrill to the world's greatest sporting spectacular, the famous Tour de France, fight your way over the Continental Divide in the action packed Aspen Alpine Race, sit in on the Mexico Olympics, our

National Championships, or bite your nails as Jose Meiffret hits 127 mph on his bicycle in his "Date With Death," and lives!

If you're more practically inclined, "What Bicycle For Touring," "How to Transport Your Bicycle by Car," "Packing for Touring," "Tandeming Techniques," "Handlebars and Riding Position," "Saddle Position," and many more informative articles are offered.

There are sections on bikeways and trails, health and fitness, cycling's golden age, feminine freewheeling, and just plain having fun.

Over fifty authors with highly divergent styles will give you, in ninety articles spanning four hundred pages, the best bike reading entertainment available.

Early Bicycles, by Philip Sumner, London, Hugh Evelyn Limited, 1966, $7.50.

In every cyclist's library there should be one book on the bicycle's colorful history. History books can be a drag, but not Philip Sumner's beautifully presented work, *Early Bicycles,* a very handsome volume of few pages but impressive quality.

The evolution of the bicycle is a fascinating story. The author follows it from its primitive forms of the eighteenth century and the first use of pedals, through the development of the 'boneshaker,' the invention of rear wheel chain-drive, culminating in the introduction of the Rover cycle and the bicycles built at the close of the Edwardian era.

The text, printed on a heavy olive green stock, is accompanied by many interesting illustrations and diagrams in the style of the period. Twelve superlative engravings, each occupying a full page (10 x 15 inches, black on white), illustrate a wide variety of historic bicycles which represent important advances in cycle design.

The visual presentation and fine lithography more than compensate for the brief text. *Early Bicycles* is more of a showpiece than a history book, yet it presents a valuable synopsis of the bicycle's development.

Definitely a collector's item (now out of print and available in limited quantity only) *Early Bicycles* is highly recommended for everyone with an interest in the bicycle's heritage and for all who appreciate an exceptionally fine example of graphic presentation.

The Bicycle Book, The Earth Action Council, UCLA, Box 24390, Los Angeles, California 90024, 1971, 56¢.

The Bicycle Book is a pamphlet (only forty-five pages) in the best tradition of that political form. Implicit from

one end to the other is an intention very similar to Tom Cuthbertson's: to dispel the myths surrounding bicycles in the U.S. and convince people to ride them.

Most of the thing involves itself with just laying out guidelines for the selection and care of your machine. The instructional sections are brief, straightforward in their praise and cryptic when it comes to recommendations. The effect is that the rider's perspective predominates, not that of a mechanic or student of the sport's history. You learn what you need to know for most one day bicycle adventures and little more.

More interesting to me is the stuff about bicycling. These are pages from concerned environmentalists. Like a lot of people, they may have come to pedaling for an ecological reason and then found it needed no such justification. Happily, the original reason is still good. So the introduction is about cars. There's a short history of bicycling and some instructions on how to help, like:

1. Get hooked; buy a bicycle.
2. Be a pusher; use your bike.
3. Encourage young people to get bikes and use them. Do this before the Detroit-style pushers get to them.
4. Tell parents that if their teenagers had good bikes they might not hitchhike.
5. Lend your bike.

And on the back cover:

Buy a car nevermore. Remember: ten on the sprocket, not four on the floor.
Wilhelm Ziege

This is probably the best book to give to someone who's wondering what all this stuff about bicycles and bicycling means or to a friend who thinks the things are toys. It's short enough to stand a chance of getting read.

The following are catalogues and booklets that are good sources of information to both the beginner and expert.

Wheel Goods' Bike Handbook Catalog, Wheel Goods, 2737 Hennepin, Minneapolis, Minnesota 55408, $2.00.

Big Wheel Ltd. Handbook of Cycling, Big Wheel, Ltd., 310 Holly Street, Denver, Colorado 80220, $2.10.

Gene Protuesi's Cycle-Pedia, Gene Portuesi, 6447 Michigan Avenue, Detroit, Michigan 48210, $2.00.

Cycling-Instructors' Guide, The Athletic Institute, Merchandise Mart, Room 805, Chicago, Illinois 60654. ●

BICYCLES

THE POWER TRAIN

by Robert Drennan

It is often hard to find a reasonably knowledgeable bicyclist who is willing to explain to you how the things work. If you find one, he will probably hang your bike from a rafter and point at what's happening as you change gears and apply the brakes. He'll suggest you try making your own repairs and adjustments, and just fiddle with the thing until you understand how it works.

This article isn't intended as a substitute for that kind of learning but as an introduction to actually making your own repairs and equipment choices. The best way of starting you on that road seems to me just pointing out some of the basic functions of a ten-speed and explaining how those jobs get done.

The sort of knowledge that is the final goal of this introduction is manipulative, that is, in the hands that do the fixing. But in order to teach your hands something, a lot of words and pictures are going to be presented. All of it is simply an explanation of what you'll see if you hang your bike up, change gears, and apply the brakes. The article is intended to try and tell you what to look for.

This should also help you understand something of what makes one system more efficient than another. It should help you decide which bike, which gear arrangement, which maker of parts, etc., you should choose. Theoretically, if you know what happens and how its done you will decide more intelligently what equipment you want to do it. You should also be better able to keep that equipment functioning at its highest level of efficiency.

If you haven't got a bike yet, the pictures will have to do for now. If you've got one, these pages will serve as so much finger pointing, showing you what to watch for when you hang your bike up, change the gears, and apply the brakes.

Between your feet and the rear wheel of a bicycle there is a series of simple machines connected to one another called the power train. These levers, cogs, and chain transfer energy from your legs to the rear tire and propel the bike. The power train is probably the most complex of a ten-speed's working parts, but its functions are simple. The confusion about it arises because there are a number of things that this part of the bike does. However, essentially, the power train takes the push and pull of your legs and applies that force to the rear wheel.

Thus, it basically consists of two gears with a chain connecting them and a means of applying inputs and outputs from that system.

The input to the system is the crank, which is a lever moving through a circle. To facilitate your foot's applying force to that lever a pedal is attached to the outboard end of it. The pedal rotates, allowing you to apply force to the inboard end of the crank from a number of different angles.

The inboard end of the crank lever is attached to a sprocket called the chain ring. Pushing on the crank rotates the chain ring.

At the rear of the bicycle a basically similar relationship exists. The rear tire is connected to levers just as is the pedal. These levers, spokes, are attached to a hub, which has attached to it a sprocket similar to that of the chain ring. The rear sprocket is called the free wheel.

The free wheel and chain ring are connected to one another by a chain. The sprockets at either end of the power train are toothed so that the transmission of power to and from the chain is not subject to loss through slippage.

As you can see, the basic pattern through which force flows in the power train is pretty simple. What makes it less so is the fact that the various parts of it are different sizes. The crank is shorter than the spokes, the chain ring is, generally, larger than the free wheel. Because of these relative differences in size, the force and motion of the pedals are changed by the time they get to the rear tire. Because the length of the spokes and cranks are constant on any full-sized bicycle they can be taken into account later on when you start to interpret all this information in terms of actually moving the bike. At this point the important relationship is that between the free wheel and chain ring.

Because the front and rear sprockets are connected by a chain, one inch of rotation at the outer edge of the front sprocket causes one inch of rotation at the outer edge of the rear sprocket. Since their circumferences differ, the front sprocket may require thirty-six inches of outer-edge movement to turn a single revolution. If the rear sprocket is only twelve inches in circumference, it will rotate three times every time the front sprocket rotates once. That is, the free wheel will revolve faster than the chain ring.

The effect of this, of course, is to produce a variety of mechanical advantages in the power train. By changing the relative sizes of the two sprockets you vary the number of turns of the crank necessary to move the bike a given distance. At the same time, you vary how much resistance the crank will present to your feet, how hard you'll have to push on the pedals in order to move the bike.

The desire for variation in mechanical advantage led bicycle manufacturers to devise systems of changing the size of the free wheel sprocket. The first such device was encased entirely in the hub of the rear wheel. The Sturmey-Archer hub of this design allows three gear ratios, all varied by changes inside the hub of the free wheel and carried off by a fiendishly complex mechanism. The drawback to such a gear changer is that it is severely limited in terms of possible gear combinations and is subject to any number of internal catastrophes.

The logical alternative to a fixed chain and movable gears is to have a number of gears on the free wheel and move the chain from one to the other. It's just this system that is used on nearly all fine touring bicycles. The job of doing so, however, creates not only the difficulty of moving the chain from one free-wheel sprocket to another but also involves the problem of taking up the slack created in the chain as you shift from a larger to a smaller sprocket.

An Italian firm, Campagnolo, designed and patented a device that moves a bicycle chain from one sprocket to another while the bicycle is being ridden. The thing is called a 'derailleur' because it 'derails' the chain from one sprocket and 'rerails' it on another. It does so by applying side force to the moving chain, bending it at a point several inches in front of the sprocket. The bent chain, since it is no longer in line with its original position, spirals or climbs out of the

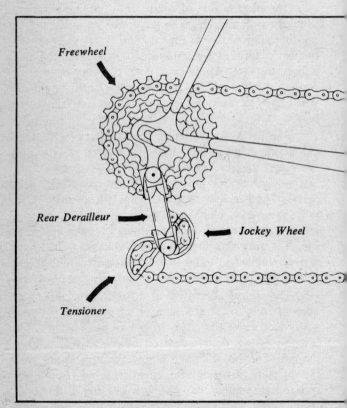

'rail' of that sprocket. The chain rises from the teeth of the original sprocket and rides on top of them. It then climbs to the next sprocket and drops into this newly selected rail. This new position is in line with the derailleur and so no bending of the chain occurs. Thus, the chain stays in its new sprocket.

As you turn the crank of your bicycle and shift the gears, you will hear first the rivets of the chain catching on the teeth of the new sprocket. If you turn the crank slowly and gradually move the derailleur, you will see

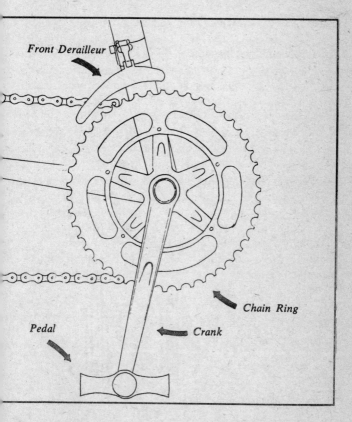

the angle of the bent chain intersect with the plane of the free-wheel sprocket. This angle of incidence spirals the chain onto the new sprocket. Most important is the fact that the teeth of the sprocket, rather than the derailleur, lifts the chain. The derailleur applies side force, bending the chain and the free-wheel sprocket lifts it as a result. Because the change is effected by the sprocket, it must be moving in order to change gears. That is, you have to pedal forward while you're shifting.

The derailleur bends the chain only a certain amount. Once the chain has moved to a new sprocket it, in effect, straightens out. The bending of the chain is controlled by the travel of the derailleur. Once the chain has moved far enough, its new position aligns with the derailleur plane. Thus, the chain, free wheel, and derailleur are in line and no more bending occurs. The chain then drops down into the teeth of the selected free-wheel sprocket.

How derailleurs derail is another matter. What is needed is a device that applies side pressure. One unusual method of doing so comes from England and is called the 'Benelux' derailleur. The Benelux is simply a horizontally mounted expansion spring which, when released, pushes a guide against the chain, derailing it.

The major problem in derailing is to apply force at right angles to the chain throughout the gear change and to do it smoothly, without uneven, jerking move-

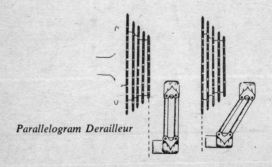

Parallelogram Derailleur

ments from the guide or cage which bends the chain. The Benelux system is subject to a number of variations in spring force and travel and so shifts sloppily. Campagnolo's original design, the one now used by all major derailleur manufacturers, solves this problem by employing a system called the 'deformable parallelogram.'

The adjective 'deformable' may be misleading. Parallelograms have the peculiar property of being able to change their shape without ceasing to be parallelograms. They 'deform' in a very controlled and specific way: The angles between the sides change and the figure 'leans,' but in so doing, it's opposing sides remain parallel to one another. In a derailleur the effect of this is that the mechanism leans into the chain applying pressure to it from a constant direction and in very controllable degrees.

Deforming or leaning a derailleur is accomplished by changing one of its angles. Modern derailleurs alter their shape through the use of a cable that runs across the diagonal of the mechanism's parallelogram which, when pulled, shortens that diagonal, changing the angles and shape of the figure.

The lean described in the pictures above shows the derailleur climbing through the cluster, from a small sprocket to a larger one. Obviously it must also be able to retreat. However, climbing down is much easier than up and the force necessary to bend the chain enough to do so is not nearly so great. As a result of this lesser resistance in climbing down, derailleurs are equipped with a return spring. By slackening or releasing the cable the parallelogram 'reforms' itself and moves the chain down through the cluster.

As you can see, the bottom side of a derailleur is the critical one. Moving it applies the force to the chain needed to bend it. Because a parallelogram maintains its opposing sides parallel to each other, fixing the top side keeps the bottom side moving in a continuous line at a constant angle to the chain as it applies derailing force. This insures that the chain will be 'rerailed' in the proper plane with the new gear.

Attached to the mobile, bottom side of the parallelogram is a cage or guide which does the actual pushing. Inside the cage is a free-turning idler wheel (kind of a toothless sprocket) called a 'jockey' wheel. It is at this point, at the jockey wheel, that side force is applied to the chain. The wheel provides a bearing point to cut friction created by the derailleur and cage as it pushes or jockeys the chain toward the new sprocket.

Changing from one gear to another varies the amount of chain necessary to reach from the free wheel to the chain ring and back. Obviously, it doesn't take as much chain to go around a small free wheel and head back towards the chain ring as it does to go around a larger free wheel. Because the tops of both the front and back gears do the pulling the slack accumulates underneath and between the sprockets. If this slack were allowed to whip around it would bend the chain as you pedaled and derail it indiscriminantly.

Mounted in the cage in front of the jockey wheel is a second idler wheel and guide similar to the jockey mechanism. This wheel is called the 'tensioner' because it takes up slack, maintaining a constant amount of tension on the chain. The cage and tensioner wheel are spring-loaded so that they apply clockwise pressure on the chain. The function of this cage and wheel is, simply, to wrap up or reel in any extra chain.

On some derailleurs the jockey wheel only jockeys the chain from side to side, derailing it. This leaves the tensioner the full responsibility of wrapping up chain. In others, the jockey wheel is pivoted on an arm and is spring-loaded so that it too will wrap up chain. The distinction depends on where it is mounted. If, as in the first diagram below, the jockey wheel is mounted directly to the parallelogram, it will not be able to reel in any of the excess chain and the tensioner will have to accommodate it all.

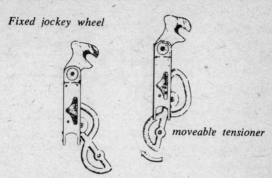

Fixed jockey wheel

moveable tensioner

If, however, the jockey wheel is pivoted at a distance from the bottom side of the derailleur and its arm is spring-loaded, it will wrap chain.

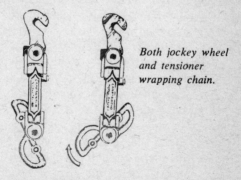

Both jockey wheel and tensioner wrapping chain.

This function of the cage mechanism can be very important on touring bicycles when wide gear ranges necessitate large differences in sprocket size. The variation in excess chain through these gears requires an effective wrapping up mechanism. If both tensioner and jockey wheel wrap chain, so much the better.

One some derailleurs, not only is the jockey-tensioner spring-loaded, but the top of the parallelogram is also enlisted. This makes it possible for the entire mechanism to move, adding to the amount of slack in the chain that can be tensioned.

DERAILLEURS

Discussing the basic principles of derailleur design is one thing; choosing among particular examples of their manufacture is another. There are a great number of variables involved in turning this relatively simple theory into an effective and reliable derailing mechanism. Among them are considerations such as the size and weight of the part and its specific methods of operation. That is, how the general principle of deforming parallelogram derailleurs is applied to a specific design. Perhaps more important are the differences in materials used and the quality of craftsmanship that goes into each piece of equipment.

Derailleurs are made on a mass-produced basis only in Italy, France, Japan, and Spain. The only Italian company is Campagnolo and the only Spanish firm is Zeus, which makes a direct copy of the Campagnolo. In fact, Zeus has infringed on international copyright conventions, but these are not recognized in Spain. France produces the well-known Huret and Simplex lines and the less famous Triplex and Gian Robert. Japan is the home of Shimano and Maeda Industries which makes the 'Sun Tour.'

The U.S. makes no derailleurs for the same reason that it makes no other lightweight bicycle parts or frames: Labor is too expensive. The construction of lightweight bikes and equipment takes a considerable amount of time and manual labor. A good illustration is the Schwinn 'Paramount,' the only top quality American-made bicycle. Although it's one of the most expensive bikes available in this country, it is a low profit item for the manufacturer despite being free of import duty and overseas shipping charges. The Paramount's frame is constructed here, the tubing that goes into the frame and all the bike's parts are foreign made.

However, because foreign labor is relatively cheap and bicycle craftsmanship something of a tradition, you shouldn't be lead to believe that all these imported derailleurs are impeccable. As in all bicycle components there is a great range in capacity and reliability. Various models are designed and built for certain purposes, and others are to be avoided altogether.

Gian Robert

Gian Robert derailleurs fit into this latter description. This model is not commonly found as a replacement part but is found on some lower-priced bikes. The stamped steel parts are crudely assembled. It has a small range and sloppy action. Both front and rear units are very difficult to adjust. Most important, the Gian Robert is prone to disintegrate with heavy use. If you have this model on your bike, and will be doing a lot of riding; change it now. It may be adequate for infrequent use, but it's just not dependable.

Favorit

Another in the less than adequate category. This derailleur is found on the 'CZ Jawa.' It's very difficult to operate because it swings unevenly through its limited range. The Favorit is as difficult to adjust as the Gian Robert. This is a very heavy derailleur. Though it is reliable compared to the Gian Robert, the cables, chain, and human legs with which it is associated are liable to suffer because of its imprecision.

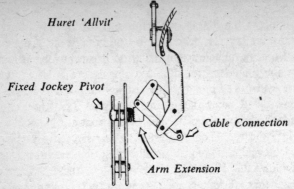

Huret 'Allvit'

Fixed Jockey Pivot

Cable Connection

Arm Extension

Huret

Huret is the standard derailleur for inexpensive five- and ten-speed bikes. The French firm makes five basic rear models, but two of them are not readily available in the U. S.

The Allvit model is very common on less expensive bicycles and can be found on many Schwinns. The Allvit is made entirely of stamped steel parts which are nicely chromed on the outside and poorly tooled where the work gets done. Like most Hurets, the cable-fastening bolts strip easily. The pivots of the parallelogram are bolted and so can come lose, causing sloppy action and, finally, lost parts. Some Hurets come from the factory inoperable due to faulty right angle bends and bad alignment; so you should check any of them before you leave the shop.

There are also a number of weaknesses of design in the Allvit. The top pivot of the derailleur has no spring and so cannot wrap excess chain. Making matters worse, the jockey wheel is attached directly to the bottom of the parallelogram so that it cannot reel in chain either. The tensioner, which must do all the slack gathering, is very short and so is limited.

The entire cage is attached to the parallelogram by an extension of one of its legs, rather than by its full

98

length. This is an especially important flaw for the tourist. This weak point is subject to bending under hard use and when shifting through the wide gaps between gears on the touring bike.

The design of the parallelogram mechanism itself is also less than ideal. On most derailleurs the top of the figure is fixed and the bottom leans into the chain. The Allvit has a heavy frame which fixes the bottom of the parallelogram so that the top of it reaches toward the chain and is used to bend it. This design characteristic limits the size of the free wheel that the Allvit can handle.

The Allvit has an unusual and welcome addition in its cable adjuster. It is also reasonably easy to limit the travel of the parallelogram with the two stop screws located on the outside of the mechanism.

All derailleurs are susceptible to sluggishness and sticking when road dirt and gunk build up in their working parts. For this reason, try to keep them clean and don't leave excess oil on them. Hurets, especially the Allvit, have mechanisms which are very closely packed

Huret 'Allvit'

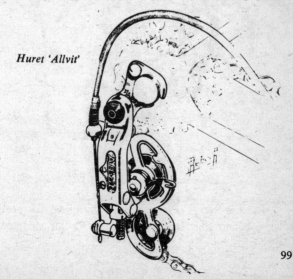

together and so they readily accumulate action-stopping dirt if there is any oil left around for it to cling to.

The Huret 'Svelto' is something of an exception to the rest of the company's line. It's a small and flimsy looking derailleur, but it's reliable and quick. It is lightweight and smooth working and has an efficient design, which uses the preferable, all riveted parallelogram. Within the limits of its intended use, it's quite nice.

The Svelto can handle wide, mountain gearing very smoothly. This would make it a suitable derailleur for touring. However, Huret's standard design involves mounting the cage to the bottom section of the parallelogram with a 90° bend in a bracket. This is something less than indestructible and so might help you develop a justified case of paranoia if you plan an extended tour.

Huret 'Svelto'

But the Svelto is a great little derailleur for around town use and short tours. Dollar for dollar its hard to buy more for your money. When new it works more smoothly than the Campagnolo 'Valentino' but it may not last so long nor break-in so well. If your bike is for errands, this and the best of the Japanese derailleurs are probably the most reasonable choices.

Simplex

Simplex is the other French manufacturer. Their equipment is famous for its extensive use of a plastic called 'delrin.' The first derailleurs made of this material were used in the 1962 Tour de France and the acetal resin has been used by Simplex ever since.

Delrin has a number of advantages. The first is that it is extremely light, about half the weight of steel. It can also be machined very smoothly and so makes an evenly operating bearing wherever it is used. For a plastic, it wears very well, but, relative to other derailleur materials, not so well at all. Major faults include its general weakness: it will simply break under pressure. It is also

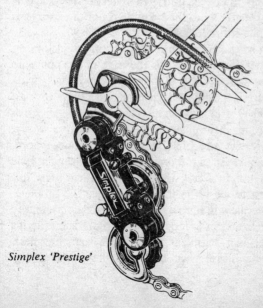

Simplex 'Prestige'

a workable material, that is, any constant force on it will eventually dent or gouge it, loosening any attachments made to it, such as spring ends.

The original 'Prestige' model made of delrin was not very sturdy and both the top line Simplex derailleurs now have steel reinforcements added to them. The only all delrin derailleur that Simplex is now making is called the 'Export' and is found only on very inexpensive bicycles. Though the Export is very smooth it reacts poorly to wide gear ranges and long use and so is not suitable for touring. This model can be recognized and so easily avoided by its white plastic parallelogram.

The new Prestige is black with a red Simplex badge. It is very light and now substantially more reliable with the addition of reinforcements. The delrin in it is very well tooled as are the few steel parts, and the whole thing is nicely assembled.

The parallelogram on a Prestige is very big and so can handle the newest six-sprocket free wheels, the largest having as many as thirty-seven teeth. The cage is attached substantially to the bottom arm of the parallelogram along its entire length.

It also has both top and bottom springs which move the whole derailleur as well as the cage in wrapping up chain. As a result, it will accommodate extremely wide ranges. There is a significant problem with these springs, however. They are secured in the delrin by 90° catch angles bent in them. These catches work the delrin, stretching it and the hole in which they are placed. Simplex goes so far as to bore a second replacement hole for you to use in fixing the worn derailleur, but this doesn't seem to me to be the way to solve the problem.

Another flaw in both of Simplex's models is the way in which their delrin components wear. As a plastic it's remarkable; as a derailleur material it's something less. The most significant wear occurs at the hinged angles of the parallelogram mechanism. The vertical sides of the figure on both the Prestige and 'Criterium' models are reinforced with chromed and anodized steel. However, the bottom and top sides are not because they are particularly massive and need no reinforcement to keep them from breaking. The vertical reinforcing braces bear directly on the delrin with every shift and in time will wear it. As a result, this bearing point becomes loose and eventually shifts sloppily. This loosening cannot be corrected because the axes on which the parallelogram pivot are press-fitted. Although this rivoting avoids Huret's problem of loosened parts, it prohibits adjustment.

If the life expectancy of the Simplex derailleurs isn't the best, the use of delrin has made them very smooth in operation. They are light, quick, and as smooth as any when new. But they don't break in, they break down, with long use.

The Criterium, Simplex's best derailleur, is very similar to the Prestige. It is finished a little more nicely than the less expensive model: There is chrome where the Prestige has anodized material, and the whole mechanism is beefed-up with thicker gauge parts.

The only significant difference, other than that the Criterium is generally stronger, is that it has a longer parallelogram travel. This makes it capable of handling large, six-sprocket touring clusters more easily.

Simplex derailleurs have a number of nice touches. They are light, have excellent action, and are reasonably sturdy. Their only real problem is their plastic parts. On a long tour, with extra weight and hard shifting, the stress on these parts can wear them significantly. Just when the shifting offers the most resistance the worn and sloppy derailleur can fail. This, of course, is only after a lot of use, and for around town riding Simplex stuff is more than adequate.

The inexpensive Japanese derailleur, the 'Sun Tour GT,' is a fine piece of equipment. It is a fairly new addition to the limited number now available. The body of the mechanism is constructed of aluminum alloy which is well-finished and massive in its proportions. Like the Shimano, it won't break. Of course, because it is made of alloy it isn't so heavy as the 'Lark' or 'Eagle,' but it outweighs most European models.

The most unusual thing about the Sun Tour is its shape. The parallelogram on this derailleur is nearly horizontal and so points forward, toward the chain ring. Most derailleurs hang straight down, deflecting the chain at a severe angle with the free wheel. The normal method restricts the amount of chain that comes in contact with the smaller rear sprockets. The Sun Tour design simply wraps more chain around the free wheel. This is especially important with small sprockets and heavy loads. If there aren't enough teeth holding onto the chain the pressure of pedaling can cause the chain to jump over the teeth.

Another curious plus of the Maeda design is the cant of the parallelogram. Most derailleurs lean their parallelograms straight into the free wheel. The Sun

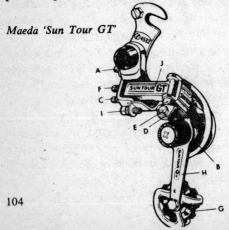

Maeda 'Sun Tour GT'

Tour's is set at an angle so that it follows the contour of the free wheel block. That is, as the parallelogram deforms it pushes against the chain in a direction that conforms with the conical shape of the entire free wheel cluster. This and the horizontally mounted parallelogram effect very smooth chain feed to the free wheel and easy shifting through the gears.

The Sun Tour's cage is similar to the Huret 'Luxe's.' The jockey wheel is fixed and the long tensioner arm must wrap all the chain. However, the Japanese derailleur has a very securely mounted cage that won't break. The tensioner cage is very well sprung and so will easily handle the chain-wrapping functions needed with touring gears. One other nice touch found here is the open cage. You don't have to break the chain to get it out of the derailleur. The whole thing amounts to a derailleur with a very wide range: 14–36—36–54.

Adjusting the limits of the parallelogram's travel is easy, as both screws are mounted in the rear, side by side. In addition to these adjustments, there is a screw setting for variation in the angle of the entire mechanism so that you can adapt the derailleur perfectly to various chain lengths and sprocket sizes. This simply adds to the contour accuracies already so pronounced in this derailleur.

The Sun Tour isn't common, but it has proven itself to be first-rate in every sense. Both it and its matching front derailleur are used in racing in Japan and Asia. (There are more professional bicycle racers in Japan than in Europe.) The Sun Tour will probably not be extensively used by European racers because Campagnolo is so well-entrenched. However, the next few years will surely see more and more high quality Japanese bikes and equipment.

This is an excellent derailleur for the economy-minded tourist. In fact, short of the Campagnolo Gran

Turismo,' you can't do better. The model is available in the U. S. now, but you may have to look for one. It is usually priced under fifteen dollars.

Shimano

The Japanese firm Shimano manufactures a number of rear derailleurs, two of which are very common on inexpensive bicycles made in the U. S. These two, the Lark and the Eagle, are very similar in design. Shimano also makes some very interesting lightweight derailleurs. The one most suitable for touring is the 'Crane GS.'

When Shimano first started making derailleurs, they produced one with two cables. Unlike modern derailleurs, which are pulled up the cluster (from the small to larger sprockets) and then return downward by means of a spring, the Shimano was pulled in both directions. This was a very sloppy system that required constant adjustment to keep the cables synchronized.

New Shimanos have one cable and a return spring. Apparently sensitive to the problems of cable stretch as a result of their experience with two of them, Shimanos are equipped with cable adjusters. This is a convenience that is found on too few derailleurs.

All Shimanos have a top spring and healthy bottom tensioner spring and ample cage. Both work well, coordinating the length of the derailleur and of the cage to wrap chain. This, and the sturdy, long parallelogram mechanism, makes them good, reliable derailleurs.

The Lark and Eagle are made of steel. The chrome work on both is up to high Japanese standards, but the stamped steel parts are poorly finished at their edges. All the material in any Shimano is indestructible, but the heavy gauge parts make the Lark a hefty 13 ounces. Even though the thing is built to bounce successfully, it often comes with a chromed steel protective arm that adds another 4.5 ounces to the whole ensemble. This arm is obviously built-in to shield the derailleur from American children, but it should certainly be removed if you're going to tour with this model. Unfortunately, the guard on the Eagle is built-in permanently and cannot be removed.

The Lark and Eagle are becoming increasingly more common on bikes in this country. They are easy to adjust; their stop screws are in easy reach and are side by side out front. They also operate smoothly. Both are highly recommended where price is more important than weight and where aesthetics is of no concern at all. In return for all that weight you get sturdiness and reliability, two important factors especially on a budget tour.

Shimano's newer series of derailleurs, the Crane series, moves them into the quality range earlier reserved for the best European models and the Sun Tour GT. The Crane GS is designed and built with the weight-conscious tourist in mind. It will handle very wide ranges and has a long tensioner arm to wrap chain. It is almost all made of alloy.

Shimano's Lark and Eagle point forward slightly approaching the advantages of the Sun Tour. The Crane series carries this step even further, mounting the body of the derailleur almost horizontally. The craftsmanship of the alloy is excellent. It is an attractive and efficient mechanism.

The Crane GS doesn't have the adjustments that distinguish the Sun Tour as a peculiarly adaptable touring derailleur but it has many design advantages. Again, from Japan, an excellent buy that delivers a more than adequate product.

Campagnolo

Campagnolo is traditionally revered as the finest maker of bicycle equipment. Their old 'Record' and the newer 'Nuovo Record' are required equipment on the bikes used in European racing. Their stuff is also found on most really active or wealthy or both riders' bikes. Campagnolo is being fitted by more and more bike makers despite being priced to the limit of what the traffic will bear.

The newest line of five rear derailleurs and two front changers includes an economy stamped steel model found on bikes as cheap as $125. This model, the 'Valentino,' is a step down from the previous tradition of superb quality. It's sturdy while not being heavy and is pretty well machined and chromed.

The Valentino has no top spring to take up chain and its cage is rather small. But it has a very long parallelogram action due to the dimensions of that figure. It will easily reach farther than a Simplex.

Most of the details of its design are sound. The jockey mechanism is attached securely, the bearings are good throughout and the cable attachment mechanism is like that on the other Campagnolo models—excellent.

The Valentino is the only derailleur Campagnolo makes that is subject to serious criticism. There are those who argue that it has a stiff action and is hard to

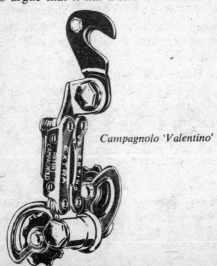

Campagnolo 'Valentino'

operate. The parallelogram mechanism has a complete ensemble of brass bushings but the derailleur is equipped with a very strong return spring. This makes climbing sometimes difficult, though there is never any problem with the thing failing to return.

Some bicyclists regard the Valentino as an adequate utility model, but one not so good as its Japanese equivalents, which are very strong and smooth. I prefer it to the even more expensive Hurets and Simplexes. It is more reliable and much stronger than either.

Campagnolo 'Nuovo Record'

The Nuovo Record, on the other hand, is beyond reproach except when you ask it to do things for which it isn't designed. This is a racing derailleur and is specifically built to handle close free-wheel clusters quickly and smoothly. It is also the best nontouring, recreational derailleur available. For $32.00 it ought to be.

Since it is not designed for touring's large free

109

wheels, it doesn't need a top spring to wrap up the extra chain needed on a mountain-geared touring bike. Similarly, it doesn't need an extra large jockey and tensioner cage. It is simply a brilliantly designed and manufactured all alloy derailleur. In fact, it is so highly regarded that some riders have a larger cage custom-made for it so that they can use it for touring. This is the dedication of an aficionado and isn't the best way to get an excellent touring derailleur.

* * * * *

All those derailleurs that have been discussed so far, though some can be used with large, touring free wheels, are basically designed for recreational and racing use. The racer demands the maximum efficiency from his bicycle and so his gear ratios are close to one another. Very small changes occur as he shifts gears. The bicycle racer is, of course, in excellent physical condition. He is also extremly sensitive to the resistance and speed of the cranks while he is pedaling. As a result, he sacrifices gearing that has a wide range in order to achieve the greatest possible speeds. He compensates for not having very low gears by being in great shape and by strictly limiting the weight of his bicycle.

The recreational, around town bicyclist can work hard getting up a hill, harder than he would be able to sustain all day, because most of his rides are short. He too has only a moderate overall range to his gears because he doesn't need more. He carries little weight and rests often.

The tourist, on the other hand, rides all day with as much as thirty pounds strapped to his bicycle. He is very likely to be climbing steep hills and sometimes even very long ones. His central concern is distance, not speed. Though the two are related, the only way to cover considerable distances with a heavy load of camping gear and spare parts is to sustain a comfortable level of activity. That means pedaling just so fast and just so hard.

In order to do that under a wide variety of conditions, whether you're headed up hill or down, into the wind or with it at your back, you must have a wide range of gears available. A much fuller analysis of this problem can be found in the chapter on gearing. For now, it is enough to know that to achieve a wide range you have to equip your bike with a free-wheel cluster that has both extremely small and extremely large sprockets.

There are two factors that determine what size free-wheel sprocket a derailleur can handle. The first is how far away from the hub of the free wheel the parallelogram reaches. The cage and jockey wheel must apply pressure to the chain at some distance from the sprocket and so must simply reach far enough away from the largest sprocket to clear its outer edge.

The second factor involves the effect on chain length of having extreme differences in the size of your sprockets. As was mentioned earlier, the cage is spring-loaded and reels in the extra chain as you shift from a large sprocket to a small one. On some derailleurs the entire mechanism is sprung so that it can shift in conjunction with the cage and reel in even more chain.

These two factors determine the capacity of a rear derailleur and are usually critical in the tourist's choice of a bike or replacement equipment. Some people take a kind of dark and stoic pleasure in groaning up hills and collapsing at night. Others opt for the wide range the ten-speed can deliver or even add a third chain ring sprocket and so have fifteen gears. If your tour is to be at all long or if your load is to be considerable you should equip your machine with a wide range of gears. If you're in lousy shape, you might change your gearing just to make things easier. There is no reason to pull hard when you can shift down and climb slowly up any hill.

Huret makes three derailleurs with large capacities. They all use the upper end 'Luxe' parallelogram mechanism but have different cage sizes.

The Huret Luxe 'Competition' is the smallest of these. It is a racing-oriented derailleur and so accommodates a gear range that is relatively small for the tourist. Huret states that the Competition will take a free wheel with the smallest sprocket having thirteen teeth and the largest having twenty-four and a chain ring with the smallest sprocket having thirty-six teeth and the largest fifty-three. You'll see this information noted on derailleurs or on their packing boxes as follows: 13–24—36–53. The outer figures, thirteen and fifty-three, express the highest gear ratio, that one you would use at top speed. For the camping bicyclist the inner numbers express a more important gear, the lowest or that one you'd use going up the steepest hill.

The Huret Luxe 'Touring' has a somewhat larger cage than the Competition and can handle a wider gear arrangement. Its capacity is 13–30—36–53. Its larger cage with a longer tensioner arm makes it capable of wrapping up more chain and so it can be equipped with a lower low gear than the Competition.

The Huret Luxe 'Super-Touring' is the top of their line. It combines the advantages of being relatively light and still having a wide capacity. Its capacity is 13–30—26–53.

The business of extending the bottom side of the parallelogram low enough to bend the chain on a large free wheel is handled in the same way on all three of these Hurets. The parallelogram itself is about the same size as that on the standard models but here it is simply equipped with an extralong mounting bracket. This re-

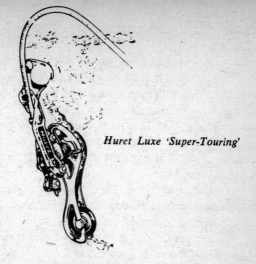

Huret Luxe 'Super-Touring'

sults in a less smoothly operating mechanism.

More important is the tensioner function of the derailleur. All Hurets attach the cage to the parallelogram by bolting it to an extension of one of the arms. In climbing the really large gaps between touring gears a lot of force is applied to this extension. At the point where one pivot of the parallelogram meets this extension there is, of course, a bearing. This thin spot is a weak link in the derailleur's construction and can be twisted out of alignment by the stresses of touring shifts.

The effect is more than inconvenient. A derailleur that is out of adjustment or twisted out of line can easily catch the spokes with resulting destruction of itself, the spokes, etc. A spoke guard helps prevent this, most of the time, but the shifts will still be poor. Anyway, you can't depend on this model for hard or extensive use or both.

The capacity of the Super-Touring model is definitely large. But, is not so great as it could be. The tensioner arm on this Huret is very long, but the jockey wheel is attached directly to the bottom of the parallelogram and so cannot wrap chain. The fact that the top pivot of the derailleur is not spring-loaded is also limiting.

The only other flaw in the Super-Touring is found on all Hurets: The jockey and tensioner wheels are not toothed. When dirt accumulates in the bearing of these wheels it can freeze them so that they will no longer spin. Unless the chain has positive contact with them so that they are forced to turn, they can remain frozen. As the chain runs over a locked wheel it can wear one edge of it flat.

Huret's Luxe models are their best. They are well-finished and nicely chromed. They are also economical, wide range derailleurs, but are not at all reliable.

Campagnolo makes the best touring derailleur. Appropriately, it is called the Gran Turismo. Among touring equipment of its kind it is the extreme in a number of ways. Touring derailleurs have to put up with a lot of stress. The long arms and great force involved in hard shifting can bend some of them. Compagnolo makes theirs entirely of steel and heavy gauge stuff at that. The effect is simple; they will not break and weigh a ton. More accurately, 15.5 ounces as compared to the Huret Luxe Super-Touring's 10.5 ounces.

Both the jockey and tensioner arms are sprung and very long so they wrap up a lot of chain. The top pivot of the derailleur is also sprung. These two factors together help give the Gran Turismo its wide range: 13–36—36–54. What's more, this wrap-up action is very smooth. The cage is equipped with a very powerful spring and its behavior at both pivots on the body of the derailleur is aided by plastic bearings.

In conjunction with this very effective chain guide and tensioner, there is a really extraordinary parallelogram mechanism. In the first place, it's huge, big enough to derail a thirty-six-toothed free-wheel sprocket. The largest the Luxe can handle is thirty. Because of this

Campagnolo 'Gran Turismo' and 'The Nuovo Record'

large design, Campagnolo includes brass bushings on either side of each pivot in the parallelogram and so the derailleur works very smoothly even over this wide range. The thing is made to very close tolerances and breaks in with use: The longer you use it, the smoother it operates.

The Gran Turismo's details are as good as its vitals. It has a cable adjusting screw on the derailleur, a real convenience on a long tour, and the machining and finish are superb. Like all Campagnolo's derailleurs it uses the most effective of the three basic cable attachment designs. This system allows extreme deformation of the parallelogram and so makes six-sprocket free wheels a matter of course.

The Campagnolo touring model is expensive, running between $24 and $26.00. But if your Huret warps a million miles from a ten-speed shop, remember how slight the difference was. It is hard to make a change

115

in a lightweight ten-speed you wish to use for touring that is as significant as adding a good wide range free wheel and a Gran Turismo.

FRONT DERAILLEURS

On ten- and fifteen-speeds there are two or three sprockets from which to choose that are attached to the crank. These chain-ring sprockets must also be changed. The principle of doing so is exactly that of the rear derailleur, except the rear takes on the entire chain wrapping function and the front has only to bend the chain. Because there are fewer gears to choose from and fewer functions involved at the front of the power train this derailleur is often called a changer.

Because the front derailleur's job is a relatively simple one, alternate means of leaning into the chain can be used. Front derailleurs are often made with very similar, if smaller, parallelogram mechanisms as in the rear. These are the smoothest and most reliable of the front changers.

However, because it is a simpler, and so less critical job, many companies manufacture these changers with push rod devices replacing the parallelogram. In general these are less accurate and not nearly so reliable as the parallelogram types.

Simplex

The Simplex 'Prestige' front derailleur is made with extensive use of delrin as are all their power train parts. Their original changer not only had a body of delrin but the clamp that held it to the frame was also plastic. This proved to be fragile and is now made of steel. The problem lingers, however, as the body of the derailleur will sometimes break even though the clamp remains whole.

Like other Simplex equipment, the delrin is well-tooled and the metal parts well-finished. It works very smoothly when new because the plastic is an excellent bearing for the push rod to slide through.

Both the Campagnolo and Simplex push rod changers share the same problem even if they do so to different degrees. The channel through which the rod

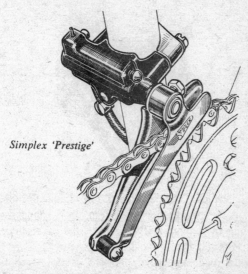

Simplex 'Prestige'

moves can become clogged and so foul the action of the changer. Both must be dismantled and cleaned in order to work smoothly. This problem is aggravated slightly in the Simplex because it is subject to wear and so holds the gunk that clogs it up better than the closer-tolerance Campagnolo mechanism.

Adjusting both is a problem as well. The outer limit to the travel of these changers is set by the point at which the cage is attached to the push rod. The inner limit is set with a stop screw that bears on the rod inside the mechanism. Adjusting both can be a fussy and inaccurate business.

Because these changers have a housing through which the rod moves they are heavy relative to parallelogram types. Even though they are made of plastic and alloy, respectively, they weigh about 50% more than those changers of the better design in the Simplex and Campagnolo lines.

Campagnolo 'Valentino'

The Simplex 'Super-Competition' front derailleur operates on the parallelogram system. It is much more reliable than their push rod but shares the shortcomings of all the French firm's plastic equipment.

Because its design is better, it works more smoothly than the other Simplex changer. Perhaps the best thing about it is that it doesn't need a superpowerful spring to compensate for an unreliable return action. The effect is that the Super-Competition is less stiff when changing than the inefficient Prestige.

The Super-Competition and the higher priced Criterium push rod changers will handle triple chain rings.

Campagnolo

Campagnolo's push rod 'Valentino' is better made than the Simplex. It is composed of alloy and steel and so is stronger. It is meticulously tooled and finished. Its more durable material gives it a longer life, but you will have to clean it periodically to get full use out of it. Like the Prestige it will hang up when dirty. Taking the Valentino apart is simple, but you shouldn't have to dismantle a derailleur periodically in order to keep it going.

Huret

Huret's Luxe and 'Standard' front derailleurs are very similar. Their all stamped steel construction makes them heavy, heavier than even the Campagnolo and Simplex push rod changers. Unlike the Simplex, however, all that weight results in a strong and reliable piece of equipment. This is the result of a very smooth working parallelogram.

It's very easy to adjust a Huret since the stop screws are conveniently placed right on top. The Luxe operates smoothly but its massive return spring offers a lot of resistance. It returns well, however, and can be used on triple chain rings. It shares with all Huret derailleurs, except the Svelto, a characteristic hinging of the parallelogram arms by means of bolts rather than rivets. Front changers don't go through the violent movement that rear derailleurs suffer so, here, loose parts are less of a problem.

Huret derailleurs are recommended for the economy-minded tourist. Among the more inexpensive de-

Huret 'Luxe'

railleurs they are an excellent and reliable value. The Huret is much lighter than the Sun Tour and more dependable and smoother than the Simplex because of its parallelogram design.

Shimano

Shimano makes a well-thought-out front derailleur that is similar in design to the Huret. There are a number of differences, however. The Shimano is also of stamped steel but of considerably heavier gauge material. Making equipment for use on sting-ray type bicycles has affected the firm's entire outlook. The thing is massive, a full 7.5 ounces. This compares with the weight of the Nuovo Record *rear* derailleur, which weighs only 8.5 ounces. The Nuovo Record front changer runs less than half the weight of the Shimano at 3.5 ounces.

The Japanese model is extremely well-tooled, all the down sides of its stamped edges have been carefully worked to remove all but the smallest imperfections.

The Shimano also compares favorably with the French derailleurs in a number of design details. Its adjusting screws are more conveniently placed than I've seen on any changer. They are side by side and, instead of being on the top of the mechanism, they stick out slightly on the left side of the bike. This makes for very easy adjustment.

Another plus that may even be unnecessary on the hefty Shimano is the way in which the jockey cage is connected to the parallelogram. This whole design issue is more important in the rear where stresses are greater and at much more critical angles, but, over a wide chain-ring range and during hard shifting it can be important. The Huret front changers connect their cages to the parallelogram in the same way as they do at the rear with an extension of one leg of the figure. As was demonstrated earlier, this is a weak point. The Shimano uses much the same system as good rear derailleurs, attaching the cage to a massive brace which is linked to one whole arm of the parallelogram. It's probably an unnecessary precaution on this already robust changer, but it works.

With this changer, the Japanese once again demonstrate their ability to incorporate good design and craftsmanship into a reliable bicycle part. Its only major shortcoming is its weight, which is certainly excessive.

Maeda

The Sun Tour front changer differs from most in one interesting design characteristic: Pulling the lever pulls the tensioning cable and shifts the chain to a smaller sprocket. Usually, on both front and rear derailleurs, the spring fulfills this function and the stronger action of your hand and the cable shifts up to larger sprockets. It seems questionable at first whether the spring could be relied on to push the chain from a small to a large chainwheel, but it seems to work beautifully. Like the rear derailleur, the Sun Tour front changer is easy to adjust and sturdy. Both are reliable and well worth their economy minded prices.

Campagnolo

The Campagnolo Nuovo Record front derailleur is very light. All its parts are made of alloy except for the nuts, the bolts, and the cage.

Aside from the usual Campagnolo efficiency, it is also excellently crafted. The finish is perfect; the legs of the parallelogram are finely shaped and tooled so as to be easy to clean and all the adjusting screws and springs are anodized. The mounting band is hinged rather than double bolted. The only advantage to this method of attachment is that only one nut may come loose since there is only one. It strikes me as a great show-off move.

The Record will easily handle a triple chain ring, shifting between even the most extreme of them quickly and smoothly. As for its life expectancy, it will last longer than your legs.

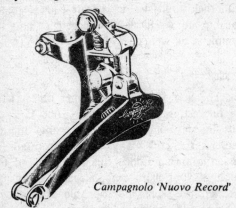

Campagnolo 'Nuovo Record'

The Record is the best front derailleur available. It is beautifully designed and crafted for long life and efficient use.

CONTROL LEVERS

Control levers are the simple machines that pull on the cable which changes the shape of a derailleur's parallelogram. They are designed like a fishing rod reel with a drum to wrap up cable and a lever attached to the drum that is used to turn it.

When shifting from a small sprocket to a larger one there is a great deal of tension on the derailleur cable and so too, on the lever and drum. The lever itself must be strong enough to endure really hard shifts. As always in bicycling, they should be as light as possible.

When you're shifting from a large sprocket to a small one you don't need the kind of force necessary to bend the chain that is needed during the harder, upward shifts. Derailleurs are equipped with return springs that move them in this downward direction. The lever must hold this spring back, keeping it from shifting down when you're in a higher gear.

In order to keep the cable taut and so restrain the return spring you have to shift the lever to a position and it must remain there. To keep it from slipping back it has a fastening screw which tightens a friction washer. The washer holds the lever where you put it.

When you're riding and shifting a lot, the movement of the levers will loosen these retaining washers. In order to keep pressure on them you should have them fitted with wing nuts or clips that can be easily tightened while you're riding. Most levers come with these thumb-screws but there are a few which have another variety that requires a screwdriver or at least a dime. These are particularly inconvenient on a long day's ride.

There is one other design factor that is important in choosing a derailleur lever. The relative sizes of the lever and the drum determine the mechanical advantage of the whole action. Levers with small drums have, in effect, a reduced gear ratio of lever movement to cable pull. This means you have to put less pressure on the lever to make it pull cable. It also means you have to move it farther to get an equal amount of cable movement. Thus, levers with small drums, like Huret's, make fine shifting adjustments easier: You can fumble around with them a bit and still set them accurately.

Control levers are most commonly located on the down-tube of the frame, either attached to a removable clip or brazed-on fittings. Some American-made ten-speed bikes and those imported from Japan are using gear levers located on the handlebar stem. This is certainly convenient for riders who use the top of the bars most of the time, but it is not much use for racing. The tourist will have to suit himself. Some find the handlebar position gets in their way and makes shifting much too difficult when they are down low on the bars.

Racing bikes are frequently found to have the levers attached to the handlebar ends, with casing running under the tape and ending at a stop where the frame-mounted levers would be. This arrangement is mainly used for races around small circuits where gear changes must be made while going through turns and in closely spaced packs of riders. The extra casing makes the shifting less exact, the cable is under more strain, and the whole arrangement is more expensive. Thus, the handlebar-end shifters are not advised for most nonracing purposes.

Levers

Simplex

The Simplex lever is very light since it uses a lot of delrin. The remaining mechanical parts are made of metal stampings, which are finished well, i.e., all their manufactured burrs have been taken off and their edges have been radiused. One other construction detail is excellent: The axle, which connects the drum to the mounting band, is very soundly crimped and will not work loose under heavy use.

The Simplex has one unusual extra—cable adjustment screws. These will easily take up slack resulting from cable stretch on a long ride. However, this factor requires housed derailleur cables.

The most significant flaw in these levers is their delrin. A great deal of stress is put on these parts especially when shifting up through wide sprocket gaps. There is a hole drilled in the lever arm where the cable

Simplex

is mounted and this weak point will break. The arms are reinforced with steel just as are the new derailleurs, but they still crack at this thin point.

Simplex levers operate very smoothly, again because the delrin used in their manufacture is a good bearing material. So good, in fact, that there is some tendency for them to slip. They have thumb-screws, however, and a good sharp twist will tighten them down or break the wings off. Their drums are about standard size, not so small as those on a Huret, nor so big as those on the Japanese Sun Tour.

Huret

Huret levers are rather heavy, but I should mention that we're talking about an ounce or so more than those made by Simplex. On the other hand, that makes them about 25% heavier.

These are all steel levers. Their construction is very good, especially at the drum axle point which is spot-welded and will probably never give out. The finish on the stamped parts is not so good, however. Many of the down sides of the cuts are still jagged. This doesn't affect the way it works as much as how it looks.

The Huret has healthy thumbscrews but this whole tensioning mechanism doesn't have friction bearings in it. The result is that you can easily tighten the movement of the levers but when you do so they won't operate as smoothly. If you loosen them to make them work

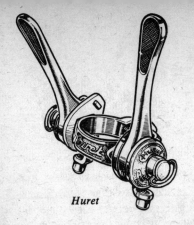

Huret

more evenly, you may have a slight problem with slippage.

The nicest thing about the Huret is its extrasmall drum. A considerable amount of lever movement results in only slight cable travel. As was mentioned before, this makes accurate shifting very easy, and is a real advantage for the novice just getting the feel of a tenspeed. There are no stop marks or clicks or numbers on a bike's levers. You have to use them and from experience feel when you're squarely in gear. Making a small change so it feels better is simple with Huret levers. What's more, not only are the drums smaller, but you can also get extra long levers that even further accentuate the mechanical advantage.

Sun Tour

The Sun Tour shifter is very heavy. It has really amazing amounts of stamped steel wrapped all over it. And then its got a really odd touch: The drums and lever arms are made of alloy, as though the company made an effort to save weight on an already much too heavy shifter. The only really good thing you can say about this lever mechanism is that it is never going to

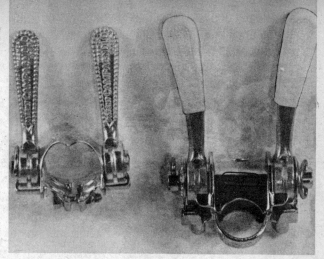

Campagnolo and Suntour Levers

break. It has one continuous steel axle connecting both drums that is about as wide as a pencil. This eliminates the need for potentially weak crimps or welds at these axle points and also turns the Sun Tour into a monster.

The Japanese lever has thumbscrews for tension adjustment and very long arms that are easy to find. It comes with friction bearings and so works very smoothly. It's just too bad it weighs twice as much as a Campagnolo lever.

Shimano

Shimano's is a very good shifter. It's only slightly overweight and the excess is the result of solid construction rather than heavy material. It has lots of well-machined alloy in its large drums and hefty lever arms It also has smooth bearing washers and so works very evenly.

The Shimano also has thumbscrews for easy adjustment. Like the Sun Tour, it has plastic sleeves over its lever arms to make your grip on them more secure. Some think this is inelegant, but it works.

For the money you can't get a better lever mechanism than the Shimano. It works smoothly and holds up.

Shimano

Campagnolo

Campagnolo specializes in making the lightest possible equipment. The arms and drums are all made of alloy and the band and other parts which must be steel have been whittled to a minimum. Theirs is a very simple, very effective lever.

Its construction is generally excellent; everything is finely radiused and well-chromed. If you stare a while, you see in it details of design that are well-thought-out and very reliable. One example is the way in which the drum axle is attached to the frame band. The Huret uses a very reliable but heavier extra plate and spot welds. The Sun Tour puts a huge and heavy single axle through their entire shifter. Simplex crimps theirs on carefully through a round hole. Not to be outdone, Campagnolo uses a square crimp so it won't rotate and won't weigh more than it has to. You find this kind of construction and design all over Campagnolo parts.

It works very smoothly because of its ample friction bearings but doesn't require a lot of tightening to keep it from slipping.

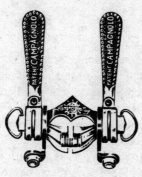

Campagnolo

The only shortcoming in Campagnolo's shifters is found in their cheapest model. Rather than thumbscrews it has the sort of adjustment that requires a screwdriver or dime. This means you have to get off the bike to adjust them. For a few cents you can get replacement thumbscrews that fit right on, but you have to go to the trouble of doing so. You can also get big nurled thumbscrews for any Campagnolo shifter that can be fitted instead of the wing type tighteners. These are the best around as you don't have to fumble for a folded-up wing nut to adjust the tension on your levers.

Campagnolo shifters are the best unless you drop something heavy on them. Short of that, they'll last forever. But unlike the Sun Tour you can't use them to drive in tent pegs. And they are expensive. ●

GEARS—
A LITTLE TEN-SPEED THEORY

By Richard B. Terry

The premise for variable gear ratios on a bicycle is that most people are most efficient when turning the pedals at around eighty to one hundred revolutions per minute. Under constant conditions this is quite comfortable with a single gear, but the land and the wind are not constant. Neither are how much weight you may carry or how tired you are. If you are tired, riding into the wind, up a hill, or with much baggage, you will find it fairly impossible to keep up the same rate of pedaling as when you were on flat ground, with a tailwind and no baggage and were feeling fresh. So the miracles of the industrial revolution bring you an assortment of gear-changing devices, most notably the derailleur, to enable you to travel at twelve to thirty-five miles per hour within this range of pedaling speed. With variation in the number and size of front chainwheels and rear sprockets, a range of gears can be chosen for a mountainous tour with baggage or for short trips on flat terrain. Just because the land around you is flat doesn't mean that ten gears are unnecessary. Flat country is notorious for winds which can bring you as close to a grinding halt as steep hills. A lot of the choosing of gear ratios and number is personal and subject to much controversy; however, I'll try to outline the problems and possibilities to make the decision more productive.

A steady rhythm of pedaling will maximize your stamina in riding. Occasional fast and slow breaks can be good to keep you loose, but constantly fluctuating the pedaling rate is an exhausting way to ride. Like an automobile engine, the body has an optimal speed of operating. Slow, hard pedaling in a high gear will move you farther per pedal stroke, but your muscles will tire and cramp easily. Pedaling too fast in a low gear, with little pressure on the pedals, is using a lot of energy in moving the legs but relatively little in moving the bicycle and you on it. In all conditions, a gear should be chosen that can be pedaled at your optimal rate without difficulty. This will generally be in the eighty to one hundred revolutions per minute range, and if such exercise proves difficult, you are out of shape and must build up to this level in low gears. (Revolutions per minute refers here to complete turns of the pedals, one revolution being two individual pedal strokes.) As a flat grade progressively steepens into a sharp hill or as you get more tired, your gear ratio will have to be gradually lowered for you to keep a smooth, rhythmic pace. Battling up a hill in high gears should be left to trained racers and those who don't have far to ride. Don't change gears more often than necessary though, for under constant conditions, this variation can cause a major break in rhythm. The advantage to derailleur shifting is that you keep right on pedaling as the gear changes, keeping the disruption of pace to a minimum.

With presently available derailleur equipment it is possible to have three, four, five, six, eight, nine, ten, twelve, fifteen, or eighteen speeds, although only five and ten are commonly found. Twelve is mostly used by racers; fifteen and eighteen, by long-distance tourists. How many do you need? When riding long distances it becomes very important to have a gear range without large gaps. In riding a three-speed, for instance, there are frequently

131

conditions in which the most efficient pedaling would be done in a gear ratio that is higher than second and lower than third. A five-speed gives you intermediate steps to fill the ratio 'gap,' but then you don't have a very high and very low gear. Ten gears may seem pretty arbitrary, but they are enough for reasonably small progessions over a large range. Further increases in the number of combinations may be for reasons of finer gradations or an increased range. But with these larger arrangements you will run into some technical difficulties to temper the benefit of extra ratios.

The five-speed is simply five sprockets on a freewheel block on the rear wheel. Sturmey-Archer makes an internal hub five-speed, but it's a complicated and sensitive mechanism that isn't made as well as their other equipment. Both of these arrangements are found mostly on the three-speed, upright handlebar models. They are better than three, but not quite adequate for varied riding. Most manufacturers of even the cheapest racing-style bikes have opted for the slight extra expense of a front changer and an extra front chainwheel so that five-speed dropped bar bikes are pretty rare. Some racers use a five for time trials, but these are races of very constant speed over flat courses. Five speeds may be all you need. but since the bike you get will probably have ten, there is little reason to remove the extras which may well prove useful.

Ten- and the rarer twelve-speed bikes have a double front chainwheel with five and six rear sprockets, respectively. With ten different gear combinations, it is possible to have a large range of ratios for extremes in riding conditions without large jumps between any two gears. This, coupled with the fact that changing is done while pedaling, provides a continuity and rhythm in pedaling that is very efficient and comfortable. Of course, all of this is only as good as your shifting habits. If you are clipping along a level road in a fairly high gear and come to a hill, don't wait until you are one hundred yards up when you can't push the gear anymore and then shift down to the lowest ratio. You will keep your speed up and your legs from overworking by smoothly shifting gears down, one by one, as the grade gets steeper. Try to keep the rhythm steady from the bottom of the hill to the top and you'll find yourself chugging up some surprising hills. The break-in rhythm caused by one drastic gear change part way up a hill is what gets a lot of people walking before the top. Smooth shifting and smooth pedaling come with practice—be conscientious at first and it will become natural after a little while. This is when cycling can become a joyful transportation.

To make all this conquering of hills possible, you must have a wide enough range of gears. The high gear, for going downhill or with strong tailwinds, isn't usually much of a problem as it is pretty constant among various manufacturers. It is the larger chainwheel in front, usually fifty or fifty-two teeth, combined with the smallest sprocket in the rear, which usually has thirteen or fourteen teeth. The low gear, the hill-climbing, wind-battling end of the range, must be checked when buying a bike. And it can vary a lot, depending on the brand. Most American bikes have a good low gear, perhaps because the bikes tend to be heavy and many Americans are not in the best of bike-riding condition. But, many European models, especially more expensive racing machines, do not go very low in the bottom end of the gear range. In the case of superlight racing bikes made for conditioned athletes, the very low gear is not usually necessary. But, sometimes it is just a case of cutting the slight extra cost of a larger rear sprocket. If the largest rear sprocket has twenty-eight to thirty-one or more teeth, the low gear will be small enough for most touring circumstances. But if the largest sprocket is twenty-four or less teeth, and the smaller front chainwheel has forty-seven to fifty teeth, the range will not be low enough for long or very sharp hills. As a general rule of thumb for people planning on doing some long riding and taking in some hills, the ratio of teeth of the smallest front chainwheel to the largest rear sprocket should be no higher than 1.5 (1½).

The gear ratio, as a number, roughly represents how far a stroke of the pedals will take you. A turn of the pedals in low gear doesn't move you and the bike as far as when you're in high. The size of the wheels also affects this so that the formula to express gear ratios has to take into account front chain wheel size, rear sprocket size, and wheel size. The formula is:

$$\frac{\text{number of teeth on chainwheel}}{\text{number of teeth on sprocket}} \times \frac{\text{wheel diameter}}{\text{(in inches)}} = \text{gear ratio}$$

The wheel diameter is in there because, for example, with a high gear of $\frac{\text{fifty-two teeth chain wheel}}{\text{fourteen teeth sprocket}}$ you will travel farther with a turn of the pedals on twenty-seven inch wheels than on twenty-six, twenty, or sixteen. The chart below shows all the possible combinations of chainwheel and sprocket sizes and enables a comparison between various ratios. These numbers are not the actual distance traveled with a revolution of the pedals. For the actual distance, multiply the gear by π (3.14). Thus the low gear of 40 will take you $40 \times 3.14 = 126$ inches or 10½ feet. A high gear of 100 will take you $100 \times 3.14 = 314$ inches or 26+feet.

Between the extreme high and low gears, there are two main ways of setting up the gear layout, which affect the order of gears as you shift. The more common system has a wide range of sizes in the rear cluster and

GEAR TABLE 27" WHEELS

	36	38	40	42	44	45	46	47	48	49	50	51	52	54
12	81.0	85.5	90.0	94.5	99.0	101.2	103.5	105.0	108.0	110.3	112.5	114.7	117.0	121.5
13	74.7	78.9	83.1	87.2	91.4	93.4	95.5	97.6	99.7	101.8	103.8	105.9	108.0	112.1
14	69.4	73.3	77.1	81.0	84.8	86.7	88.7	90.6	92.6	94.5	96.4	98.3	100.3	104.1
15	64.8	68.4	72.0	75.6	79.2	80.9	82.8	84.6	86.4	88.2	90.0	91.8	93.6	97.2
16	60.8	64.1	67.5	70.9	74.2	76.0	77.6	79.3	81.0	82.7	84.4	86.1	87.7	91.1
17	57.2	60.3	63.5	66.7	69.9	71.5	73.0	74.6	76.2	77.8	79.4	81.0	82.6	85.7
18	54.0	57.0	60.0	63.0	66.0	67.5	69.0	70.5	72.0	73.5	75.0	76.5	78.0	81.0
19	51.2	54.0	56.8	59.7	62.5	64.0	65.4	66.8	68.2	69.6	71.0	72.5	73.9	76.7
20	48.6	51.3	54.0	56.7	59.4	60.8	62.1	63.4	64.8	66.1	67.5	68.8	70.2	72.9
21	46.3	48.9	51.4	54.0	56.6	57.9	59.1	60.4	61.7	63.0	64.3	65.5	66.8	69.4
22	44.2	46.6	49.1	51.5	54.0	55.2	56.4	57.7	58.9	60.1	61.4	62.6	63.8	66.2
23	42.3	44.6	47.0	49.3	51.6	52.8	54.0	55.2	56.3	57.5	58.7	59.9	61.0	63.4
24	40.5	42.7	45.0	47.2	49.5	50.7	51.7	52.9	54.0	55.1	56.2	57.3	58.5	60.7
25	38.9	41.1	43.2	45.4	47.5	48.6	49.7	50.8	51.8	52.9	54.0	55.1	56.2	58.3
26	37.4	39.5	41.5	43.6	45.7	46.7	47.8	48.8	49.8	50.9	51.9	53.7	54.0	56.1

GEAR RATIOS NOT SHOWN ABOVE MAY BE CALCULATED AS FOLLOWS

$$GEAR = \frac{Number\ of\ teeth\ on\ C/ring}{Number\ of\ teeth\ on\ Sprocket} \times Diameter\ of\ rear\ wheel\ in\ inches$$

Reproduced from text made available by Campagnolo.

fairly closely sized front chainwheels. This way the shift from one to another chainwheel makes a jump halfway between a shift from one to another rear sprocket. For instance, here is the chart for forty-seven- and fifty-two-teethed chainwheels used with a rear cluster of fourteen, seventeen, twenty-one, twenty-six, and thirty-one teeth:

	14	17	21	26	31
52	100	83	67	54	45
47	90	75	60	49	41

With this arrangement, if you start riding in a gear of sixty and want the next highest, simply shift the front shifter from the smaller to the larger chainwheel. The next consecutive shift from sixty-seven to seventy-five means changing the front shifter down and the rear goes to the next highest (smaller) cog, seventeen. This way you can select most of the range with just the rear shifter, but for more continuous shifting it is necessary to use both front and rear at every shift.

The other arrangement is to use a relatively close range on the rear cluster, and have a big difference in the size of front chainwheels. Rear sprockets of fourteen, fifteen, seventeen, nineteen, and twenty-one can give a pretty wide spread of ratios if used with front chainwheels of thirty-eight and fifty-four. The chart would look like this:

	14	15	17	19	21
54	104	97	86	77	70
38	73	68	60	54	49

In this pattern, the single gear jumps usually require only shifting the rear derailleur. Shifting the front changer will make the jump from the high range to the low range, and within these ranges all the shifting can be done with one shifter. The slight overlap that can be seen in the above example is not entirely useless.

It provides some continuity to the two ranges and gives a closer spaced set of gears in the sixty-eight to seventy-seven range which is used for much riding in 'average' conditions.

There is the possibility of some gear arrangements in between these two methods. However, widely spaced rear clusters used with widely spaced front chainwheels are more likely to wind up with repeated gears. For instance, fourteen, seventeen, twenty-one, twenty-six, and thirty-one in the rear used with fifty-two and forty-two in front will give ten combinations. But working them out on a gear chart shows that there are four pairs of repeated ratios, so that the bike is effectively a six-speed. Yet this factor can be found on even some very expensive bikes. The other problem with some of these intermediate arrangements is that shifting a single gear jump will always require shifting both levers, sometimes shifting one in front and two in back. This is an unnecessary break in the rhythm and makes it more difficult to keep track of what gear you're riding in.

It is wise when buying a bike to count teeth, make up a chart with the gear chart or slide rule and see that the gearing is satisfactory for your purposes. You may want a wider, higher or lower range, or there may be repetitions. There are some stock ranges in sprocket clusters, though some bike shops can make up custom arrangements of sprockets. Try to make these calculations before you buy a bike so that a trade in on new equipment will be easier.

The fifteen- and eighteen-speed bikes are like the ten and twelve with the addition of a third front chainwheel. Generally it is a small one on the inside which gives some ultralow gears for mountainous travel. There are some problems associated with this addition, and for this reason Peugeot and some other companies have withdrawn their fifteen-speed models. In traveling from the outside chain wheel to the inside sprocket or the inside chain wheel to the outside sprocket, the chain has to cut across a very uncomfortable angle. Friction and the tendency to derail are both high. The chain is likely to rub on the front changer cage and the side of the rear roller cage. These two positions are also the extremes in chain tension and slack, which taxes the rear derailleur capacity. Since these extreme crossovers are neither the highest nor lowest of the ratios, it is best to avoid using them altogether. The main purpose of the extra chainwheel is not so much to give you five extra gears as to provide you with the more extreme range necessary for touring in very tough conditions. All five sprockets can be used with the middle chain wheel but stay with the outside three or four with the outside chainwheel and the inside three or four with the inside one. This means you are back to an eleven- or thirteen-speed and it may not seem worth the trouble. It is tricky to align and adjust for triple chain wheels. However, many experienced long-distance tourists use them constantly. For mountainous conditions, especially with baggage, the small inside chain wheel can provide you with a set of very low gears for climbing, high gears for descending, and a larger middle range for flat country. If your requirements are not so demanding, simplicity and expense would indicate staying with the ten-speed.

If you are going to use the triple chain wheel, most front changers can be adjusted for it, except the Campagnolo 'Valentino.' Make sure that the rear shifter can handle the capacity of chain or don't use the combinations that it won't. (This advice also goes for very wide range ten-speed arrangements.) Rear derailleurs will frequently indicate, in literature or on the mechanism, the total capacity. Some of the advertised ranges are as follows:

Make	Maximum Rear Range	Maximum Total Capacity (Front + Rear)
Simplex Prestige	13–28	37
Huret Allvit	13–28	28
Huret Svelto	13–28	32
Campagnolo Nuovo Record	13–30	32
Campagnolo Gran Turismo	13–36	43
Sun Tour GT	13–34	40

Some of these derailleurs are under great strain when used at their advertised limits. Again it is wise to avoid such combinations. See the article on derailleurs for a more complete account of capacity of the best shifters for various purposes.

To give you a feeling for what the gear ratios represent, I could tell you roughly but it's more interesting and useful to count the teeth on your bike and figure them out by equation or on the table. Get a feeling for the given gear relative to other gears or other bikes and in various riding situations. (On a three-speed hub gear, the ratio only holds for second. The Sturmey-Archer is 25% lower in first and 33% higher in third.) 100 is usually around the top of most bikes' range and is a very heavy gear indeed. 90 is a more commonly used

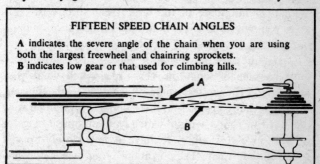

FIFTEEN SPEED CHAIN ANGLES

A indicates the severe angle of the chain when you are using both the largest freewheel and chainring sprockets.
B indicates low gear or that used for climbing hills.

high gear; 80, for when you're clipping along, maybe with a tailwind. 60s and 70s are the most used midrange for most riders. 40s and 50s are for hills. Gears below that are for mountainous grades, perhaps if you are carrying baggage. The gears you find comfortable will depend a lot on physical conditioning and the weight of the bike. In figuring out the gears you want to use, a rule of thumb is that one tooth difference in the rear sprockets is about equal to two teeth difference in the front—a little more in high gears, fractionally less in low ranges. Play around. There is enough gearing flexibility possible to eliminate most of the need for fifteen speeds. Some places can build up custom combinations or rear sprockets at little or no extra charge. The matter only entails screwing the sprockets on and off the body of the freewheel, although a special holding tool and extra sprockets are required. Get a good free wheel, like a Cyclo or a Regina, since many of the cheaper ones tend to freeze or fail in the pawls. Wide varieties of chain wheels can be installed, too, though it is frequently difficult to find ones that will fit your existing equipment. The Campagnolo is easy to get and has a range of 42 to 56 as does the Stronglight cotterless model. T.A. is harder to get hold of, but has a super-wide range for any tourist, from twenty-six teeth up. With that and some of the larger rear sprockets available, you can have a less than one to one ratio for hauling full camping gear up the Rockies comfortably.

If you start playing with your gear-arrangements, have an idea of what the gears mean and what your needs are. The easiest thing to change is the cluster, which normally costs around six dollars. First determine the narrow range within which you do most of your riding, since it is good to have a few closely spaced gears in that span. Then examine your needs for low and high gears, depending on your strength and the terrain on which you intend to ride. Look to the gear chart for what sprocket sizes will give you those extremes given the chain wheels you already have. For instance, to get a 40 to 100 range starting with chain wheels of 47 and 52 teeth, you'll need a small sprocket with 14 teeth for the high gear and a large sprocket with 31 for the low. Then select intermediate sprocket sizes which should be more widely spaced in the larger ones. A cluster of 14, 17, 21, 26, and 31 has jumps of 3, 4, 5, and 5 teeth but makes a very even range from the low to the high. The chart for this gearing is given earlier in this article. For a similar range with some closer spaced intermediate gears, you might substitute sprockets of 20 and 25 teeth or a small chain wheel of 48. In any case, double check for repeated ratios. Once you are in condition and can really use gears, there is no reason for you to feel limited by what came on the bike. And if you aren't in good condition, it is all the more important to have a wide enough range to make cycling easier. ●

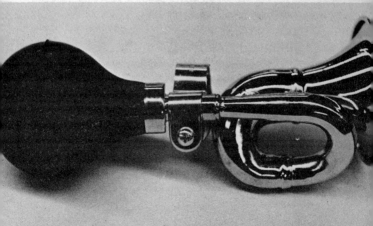

CARRYING
THE
LOAD

by William Yeuf

Walking and bicycling are about the only really efficient forms of self-propelled motion. They are very simple and regular techniques that have a lot in common in terms of pace and conditioning. But walking, in effect, is a series of stumbles by comparison to the well-oiled motion of a rider who enjoys a practiced cycling technique. The walker lifts himself and his load with every step and then drops it all in order to take another. He works against gravity, not friction, and if you watch someone walk you'll see how persistently he drops his weight only to have to pick it up again. This vertical motion has nothing to do with getting from one place to another.

A bicyclist has only the weight of his legs and sometimes that of his chest and head to lift. He minimizes this vertical business and converts his strength into horizontal thrust. Very clever.

On tour, all this means that a cyclist can go farther, faster, and with less effort. It could mean that he can carry much more, but generally, he carries a load weight even smaller than the hiker's. Often a biker's dunnage hovers around thirty pounds, plus the weight of his bicycle, but it is rarely greater than that on tour.

Of course, bicycling isn't a simple and clear-cut evolutionary advance. On a bike, it's easier to fall over. In fact, if you stop, it's almost certain this balanced wonder will fall down and you'll have to pick it up. Picking up a bicycle and its load is much less efficient than walking, and this doesn't begin to estimate the energy and good humor you lose due to injury. If you're sprinting along at a reasonable clip and you drop it, you'll find that the shortcomings of the pedestrian are suddenly much more inviting.

The more weight you carry, the fewer miles you can go, and the more precarious the condition of your bicycle. Regardless of how carefully you select from among the lightest weight camping equipment, you have to consider the difficulties of pedaling it around. Following the maxim that bringing only the essential along won't solve the problem entirely. How you load the extra weight is going to have a big effect on how far you go and whether or not you're going to be periodically lifting the whole lot of it.

For many years Americans insisted that walking, if not more efficient, was at least more noble than pedaling. They invested millions of dollars on lightweight and durable equipment that made it possible for a walker to carry as much as fifty or sixty pounds in relative comfort and stability. Perhaps the most incredible efforts were made on behalf of those who had absolutely no interest in getting anywhere—the mountaineers. Rock climbers and mountaineers take a whole lot of stuff, tote it almost purely vertical distances, and then bring the load back down again. Incredible.

But lately the bicycle has ceased to be a toy. Horizontal motion is gaining in popularity as a sport as well as a necessity and so it's starting to be taken seriously. Why good equipment and techniques have to start this way, for fun, is beyond me, but thanks to the realization that bicycling is fun as well as good sense, some fine lightweight accessories are being manufactured. This is a wish-book article on that equipment. It's included in this book so that you can see just how far touring has come. Even if you can't afford any of the three very fine sets of panniers and bags that are mentioned, you can take pride in knowing that nylon is not the sole property of the walker and climber. We've made the pictures really big so that you can study the details of this costly stuff and argue intelligently with your friends who walk. Take heart; when your ship comes in, you can buy a set of these.

The rationale behind nylon is simple. It's stronger

than cotton and so less of it will put up with more stress and abuse. The net effect is a more durable and much lighter piece of equipment. Weight, of course, is a very important consideration in biking. It has a great effect on how much distance you can cover and how stable your precarious vehicle is, especially at low speeds.

There are also other factors to really good pannier design. The convenience of your access to the load and your ability to distribute the weight in your bags is very important too. The best equipment satisfies all these needs and so improves your riding stability and the ease with which everything is sorted out when you load and unload the bike. Don't underestimate the problems of losing things right there in front of you. A great pile of tangled dunnage is nowhere to start looking for something after a long day's ride. Equipment that isn't conveniently subdivided will detract as much from your good spirits as from your stability and safety. In other words, you've got to have the whole mess organized by thing and by weight or it's going to be a drag.

As with any piece of equipment that will be involved in a long tour, panniers and bags deserve thought and practice in the way you use them. Pretour riding is usually thought of as a means of tuning up yourself and your bike. It shakes down flaws in your bicycle's component parts and teaches you how to deal with weight adjustments. But you should also be familiar with other techniques, such as loading and unloading your dunnage quickly and accurately. Just as setting up a tent or cooking over a lightweight portable stove is something you have to learn, so too do you have to become practiced in this business of weight distribution. Try weekend practice tours or simply day-long rides with all your gear aboard. It will not only strengthen your body and get you used to accommodating the very different weight relationships of a fully loaded bike but it will also teach you

145

how to hang all that stuff on properly.

Probably the first thing you'll notice is that where you locate your gear has a considerable effect on the bike's handling. Your own weight, of course, is very important. But you aren't deadweight. You can shift your body to react to changes in conditions. Your load is deadweight and just hangs there, dumbly, without a care for the effect its swaying and bouncing is having on the rest of the system.

Certainly your first consideration should be striking an acceptable balance from side to side. Every sort of loading equipment is balanced this way, but if you put all your heavy things on one side, they're going to lean the bike. That fact is simple and obvious, but if you don't think about it while you're loading the machine, you and the plane of the chain ring may be operating at slightly different angles. The repercussions of working to balance the bike as well as to move it are very real. To begin with, you might work one side of your body slightly more than another. Then your stability, will be lessened, and steering and braking are never quite the same.

146

Less obvious is the problem of setting the machine up so that there is a reasonable balance fore and aft. Too much weight piled on the rear end will make the bike's balance particularly precarious. Hang some of this added load in front-end bags. Panniers that hang on either side of the front wheel and handlebar bags of various sizes are available. Though they make steering stiffer and detract somewhat from the manuverability of the machine, the added stability they offer is well worth it. Low-speed riding, especially in traffic, is sometimes dangerous with a sluggish front end. But it's worse if the machine is all rear loaded. The gains made possible by better balance make the trade off well worth it in these situations.

Moving some of the weight forward does more than simply balance the bike fore and aft. If the considerable bulk of a full camping outfit is strapped to the rear, behind the saddle, it will have to be stacked high. Vertical proportioning of weight is the most important factor in loading and the kind of rear-end tower that results from putting everything aft will make your ride much too top heavy. Remember, dead weight won't react. Dunnage that is strapped to the machine is, in effect, part of the frame and so adds to its inertia. If you try leaning through a turn and run across some sand, you'll learn how immobile a heavily laden frame can be.

Before getting further into the problem of the vertical distribution of the load let me say this: A bike that has fallen over is usually grasped at the seat and handlebar stem and then lifted. This makes the bike a lever, the fulcrum of which is the point at which your bent rim and tire touch the ground. The distance from the fulcrum to the seat is the input arm. The distance from the fulcrum to the load is the output arm. The shorter the output arm, the easier it is to lift the load after you've dumped it. If you insist on this practice you might as well be walking, but at least make the matter as easy as possible.

This means keeping your weight low.

Keeping the load low is more important than simply making righting your machine easier. It may help even those with inner ear problems to stay up. The lower the center of gravity of your dunnage, the more likely your bike will remain vertical. This tip helps; so practice it. Not only should you pick equipment that keeps the weight low, but you should also load your heaviest things in the bottom of your bags.

There are a number of different panniers and bags that can be fixed to a touring bicycle. If you are headed for a long tour, you may have to employ a combination of them. Remember this business of vertical weight distribution when you're buying and concentrate on luggage capacities that hang low. Similarly, when you are loading your gear; you should divide the bags well so that you can proportion the weight as you see fit. This loading business will be a trade off between convenience and optimal weight relationships. There is no reason to combine your mess kit and clean clothes in a single pocket. But tools and spare parts of some kinds should be kept as low as possible. Your sleeping bag, though relatively bulky, is very light and should go on top.

There are four conventional kinds of bags used in touring. The one always used (with or without some or all of the others) is the saddlebag. It's usually rather large, but if you have really big panniers, it may not be. The saddlebag has two straps which loop through fittings provided at the rear of the saddle and a third strap which fastens the bag securely to the seat post. The body of the bag will hold a lot of gear and sometimes it has side pockets as well. These small compartments can be filled with items that have to be available in a hurry or that may be needed during the day. Patch kits, first aid kits, and cameras are often carried here.

Panniers are hung on either side of the front or rear

wheel. Those at the back are always larger and are usually employed to carry the bulk of the load. The carrier racks for rear panniers are bolted to the cycle frame below the saddle or, ideally, to specially attached, brazed on fittings. They also bolt to the frame at the lower ends at the rear spindle on each side. There are carriers that are clamped to the seat stays but these are not recommended as they slide down gradually and rest on the brake.

The size and positioning of rear panniers makes them the best luggage facility for the camping tourist. If you have any appreciable amount of weight and want to keep it low, these will do the trick. You should be careful, however, that your heels don't rub against them as you pedal.

Front pannier bags are used with a smaller carrier fitted over the front wheel in a similar way. They are favored by some riders as an alternative because they are more accessible when you are on the road and distribute the weight more evenly between the front and rear of the cycle. This is a matter of personal preference. Many campers, of course, carry both sets of bags simultaneously. You may find this necessary but you should try to avoid it. It's easy to fill whatever bags you can afford but you must remember you have to pedal all that stuff around.

Handlebar bags strap to the handlebars and to the head tube. They are very convenient for carrying items such as food and maps, which may be needed periodically during the day. Generally, these bags are small, although some larger ones, with side pockets, are available. Many good bags have a transparent map-holder along the top for easy reference as you ride. Also, for convenience's sake, you should look for a top flap that opens easily when you are in riding position. Flaps that open toward you can be difficult.

Any bag should be carried so that it won't interfere with the work of the bike. This is a critical factor in handlebar bags as they are near the wheel, brake cable, and your hands. They will only rarely hinder the operation of the brake, but the action of the cable and a ride over less than smooth roads may wear a hole in the bag. You might also fit the handlebar bag to a parallel extension of the handlebar itself. This will keep it away from your knuckles when you are on the tops of the bars.

Gerry

With this general introduction to weight on a bike taken care of, the wish-book section proceeds. Gerry's equipment is a very effective spin off from their back-packing bags. The panniers and touring pack both employ the 'CWD' system that has made Gerry's backpacks famous. This design allows you to put the load where you want it by dividing the whole bag horizontally. The resulting compartments are not only useful in proportioning weight vertically but they also make getting at what you want much easier.

150

The panniers carry to an extreme the reasonable limits of controlled weight distribution. They are well-made and, of course, much lighter than those of leather or cotton. They are made of six-ounce waterproof nylon duck and are reinforced at stress points for long wear. Their color is blue.

The touring pack is a handlebar bag. The thing is shaped like a teardrop to keep the bag stable and the weight in it as low as possible. This shape also keeps it from rubbing your hands but you should use the spacer cross bar mentioned earlier. This bag is also six-ounce blue waterproof nylon duck. The straps that attach it to the bike are leather and there is a synthetic stiffener insert that helps maintain the shape of the pack.

The panniers cost $30.00 and the pack $15.00. They are available only through retailers selling Gerry's backpacks; so you probably won't find them in a bike shop. If you'd like to have some anyway, a few of the retailers specializing in lightweight camping gear are listed. Eastern Mountain Sports has a very fast mail order delivery of these bags and other lightweight touring gear.

Gerry Bicycle Panniers and Touring Bag

Bellwether Saddlebag

Bellwether Grand Touring Panniers

Bellwether Handlebar Bag

Bellwether

This is a small company that specializes in light-weight nylon touring bags. Unfortunately, their stuff isn't very well known as yet but more and more dealers are carrying these bags.

The Bellwether touring equipment was tested thoroughly for some time by bicycling students bound for New York from San Francisco. They wrote back to the office with praise and criticisms and these well-designed bags are the result.

Special consideration was given to the stability of

the bag on the bike. If you must have deadweight, at least have it securely fastened. You can manhandle the machine a bit and so the load ought to react to this limited move by staying firmly grounded to the frame. Bellwether's prototype was secured to the rear rack with heavy snaps. These have been replaced with high quality buckles and strapping so they sit firmly behind you.

It is possible to make a pannier too big. Of course, you can also make it too small for a camper. Bellwether offers two sets. The larger one has a very nice touch that has been added since the first models. You used to stuff your sleeping bag inside the panniers, in the top compartment. Bellwether has now anchored four short straps, with two grommets in each one, on the top of the panniers. This allows room for even the most bulky gear inside and the sleeping bag can be tied with nylon cord to the top.

On their handlebar bag and small touring pack Bellwether has used 'Velcro' as a closure. This makes getting in and out of the bags very easy and is important as these compartments get frequent use.

The 'Grand Touring Pack' costs $30.00, the smaller one runs $20.00, the roomy handlebar pack is $12.50, and the saddle pack is a mere $6.00. Schwinn may be distributing these bags in 1972 and so they will be much easier to find. If you have no luck at dealers, mail order through Bellwether:

> Bellwether
> 1161 Mission Street
> San Francisco, California 94103

The Touring Cyclist Shop

Hartley Alley got sick, one long tour of Europe, of clumsy and inefficient panniers, so he designed and made his own. The resulting 'TC Panniers' are beautifully made and well-designed.

The panniers come off the bike quickly. Ten seconds will do it. Once off, they zip together for carrying by hand or shoulder strap and won't flop around loosely. The shoulder strap to fit is included with the bags at no extra charge.

On the bike, these panniers are cleverly hung from the carrier with top hooks and a bottom spring. This nifty suspension-type setup keeps the bags from jars and wobbling. The bags are made of eight-ounce waterproof rip-stop nylon. There are a total of ten compartments and all the zippered closures are covered for weather protection.

One other thing: These bags come apart. One-half of them can be attached to a rucksack frame and used very nicely for backpacking.

The 'TC Panniers' cost $46.50 a pair, postpaid. You should allow three weeks for mail order delivery to get them before you take the plane to Alaska.

The Touring Cyclist Shop
Box 378
Boulder, Colorado 80302

TC Panniers (Patent Pending)

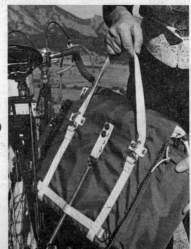

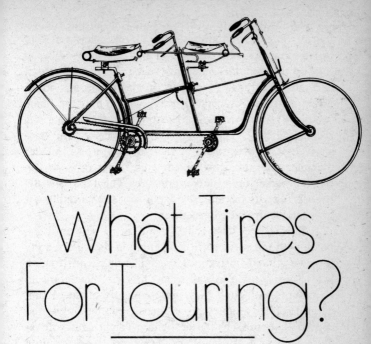

What Tires For Touring?

by Richard B. Terry

Tires are very important. They keep you from getting shaken to pieces by road vibration and they keep you on the road in wet conditions and when cornering. Tires do this most effectively when an air-inflated tube is enclosed in a strong, flexible fabric casing, which in turn is covered with rubber of a patterned surface for better road adhesion. The soft, flexible nature of tires makes them more vulnerable than other parts of the bike, and they are (usually) the only part that is in direct contact with the road. Obviously, it's a good idea to choose your tires with some thought and take care of them once you have them. But, many people don't and they usually suffer for it.

The common bicycle tire, found on all but racing-touring bikes and children's sidewalk bikes, has a base of canvas that is rubberized inside and out. The rubber is thickest around the outermost circumference where it becomes the tread. It is open on the inside and in its inside edges are embedded heavy wires (thus the name 'wired-on' which is used to distinguish them from the racing variety.) These two wires, or 'beads,' fit onto shoulders in the groove of the rim and are of smaller diameter than the rim's outside edge. Thus they contain the tube when it is under pressure. The tube is butyl rubber, fairly thick, and of low porosity so that refilling it with air is infrequently required.

Racing tires, also called 'tubulars' or 'sew-ups,' dispense with the wires and the opening in the outer casing is sewn closed instead. This single-unit construction leads some people to call them 'tubeless.' Tubulars do have tubes, although they are frequently made of thin natural rubber which is more porous than the butyl used in wired-on tires. Thus, the lighter weight tires will require refilling every few days. The fabric base is cotton or silk, not woven but rather made of two layers of parallel threads in a cross-ply arrangement. A light rubber solution is applied during manufacturing and keeps the threads from separating. Most tubulars have the heavier rubber coating only where the tread is, thus the white sidewall appearance. When looking at a tubular tire off the rim, you will find the stitching hidden behind a protective strip of fabric that is glued on.

The rim used with the tubular tires is different. There is just a shallow hollow to which the tire is glued as opposed to the deep, shouldered channel that wired-on tires are fitted into. The two styles of rim and tire are not interchangeable. Putting wired-on tires on tubular rims is completely impossible. Fitting a tubular to a wired-on rim is not only dangerous but also damaging to the tire. Also, tubulars use the thin 'Presta' valve which controls the air pressure and relies on a lock-nut to keep the air in. Virtually all wired-on tires have the wider 'Schraeder' valve which is spring-loaded.

Wired-on or Clincher

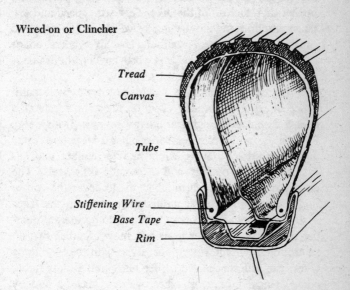

Tread
Canvas
Tube
Stiffening Wire
Base Tape
Rim

Tubular

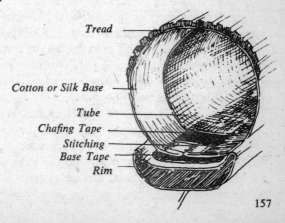

Tread
Cotton or Silk Base
Tube
Chafing Tape
Stitching
Base Tape
Rim

Each of these methods of construction has distinctive qualities. Tubular tires are for the specialist. They and the rims that fit them are very light. This is a prime consideration for riding at speed, since the revolving weight of the wheels is thus traveling faster and farther than the rest of the bike. This extra speed and distance amplifies the importance of weight in the tires and rims in terms of energy output. The bike racers' adage that an ounce on the wheels is worth two on the frame is almost exactly the case.

An extreme example will demonstrate the significance of revolving weight. Two bicycles are accelerated over a distance by identical energy sources. Both weigh 20 pounds, but bicycle number one has a 16-pound frame and 4 pounds of wheels, while bicycle number two has a frame of 18 pounds and 2 pounds of wheels. The energy required to push number one to cover the course in 20 seconds will push number two through the traps in 19.1 seconds. The energy required to accelerate number one to 20 miles per hour will move number two up to around 21.7 miles per hour. Even with these extreme cases, the differences are rather marginal. But they become critical in a sport where victory may be had by inches after a race of 150 miles. Tubular tires for the road range from 8 to 15 ounces, compared to the wired-on which are commonly in the 20 to 25 ounce range. Some track racing tires are as light as 4½ ounces but only last for a few races on even the best of tracks. The rims for tubulars weigh from 7 to 15 ounces, whereas the wired-on variety run from 18 ounces for aluminum to a more common weight of 30 ounces.

A couple of pounds of revolving weight can be saved by using tubulars, but with this lightness comes fragility. They are easily cut by sharp rocks or glass. When riding tubulars, try to get into the habit of keeping half an eye on the road surface as well as on the scenery. After a while you will learn fairly automatically to spot and avoid potholes and miscellaneous road garbage. This is the way that tubular tires can be made to last. Wired-on tires, with their heavier rubber and canvas construction, can be ridden over gravel and a lot of other impediments without much worry.

Tubulars are more sensitive in two ways. For one, their light rims are easier to dent and warp, and the narrower cross section of the tire offers less protection than does the wired-on. Thus, don't ride up curbs unless they are less than an inch high. Avoid riding over large objects like stones, branches, or sudden bumps. (Extremely large objects like mountains are usually gradual enough to ride over!) And note especially that potholes and slotted sewer covers eat wheels. Usually it is easiest to stop or ride around these obstructions. Many racers have learned to jump them, which you can do if you use toeclips and straps and show a little care at first. Push in the air and pull the bike up after you by the pedals and bars.

The dents that a rim picks up by hitting curbs, etc., cannot be worked out by adjusting spokes. Sometimes they can be hammered but the final product isn't very satisfactory as the hammered section will pull unevenly on the brake blocks. Hitting large objects damages the tubular by pinching it between the rim and road. The casing does not easily fracture at such times, but the thin inner tube frequently leaks afterwards. If the casing does go, you have a blowout. Your chances for getting a pinch cut are tremendously increased if the tires are underinflated.

The other sensitivity of tubular tires is to small sharp obstacles. The casing and tread is very thin, and at high pressures it becomes increasingly vulnerable. European racers use tubulars over very rough conditions, but they frequently change. The heavier (twelve to fifteen ounce) tubulars are somewhat more resistant to puncture, but you must still take the same kind of care of them. If you ride over broken glass, you're probably in trouble. Even if you don't get an immediate puncture, the tread probably picked up some small pieces which may work themselves in before long. This is a very common kind of puncture and can also occur with pieces of sharp rock or metal. This problem can be reduced by using tire-savers, which are simple wire and plastic tube (or other kind of spring) arrangements that brush lightly on the tire tread, knocking most of the road junk off. These are hard to find in many places, but can easily be homemade. Otherwise, brush your gloved hand lightly on the tread occasionally, especially after riding through a patch of grit. All of this may sound like a terrible nuisance, and a lot of people have troubles with tubulars until they begin to understand their unique character. But after a while most of this extra effort becomes second nature. The little care will pay off.

There is tremendous variety to tubular tires, which differ in design, quality, weight, and price. Some of these characteristics are closely linked with each other. As the prices rise from around six dollars to over 20 dollars, the tires get lighter in weight and finer in quality. Generally, a more expensive tire is not only lighter but better made and will last longer than a cheaper, heavier one. Silk casings, which are found in the more expensive types, create a stronger tire that will hold more pressure. Silk tubulars do not require the aging or curing that is recommended for cotton. Storing a cotton tire for a year or so in a cool, dark place allows the solvent used in manufacture to evaporate so that the tire will be sturdier when it is used.

Another variable is the tread design. Track racing tires usually have nothing but a smooth surface which provides ideal adhesion with the constant conditions of

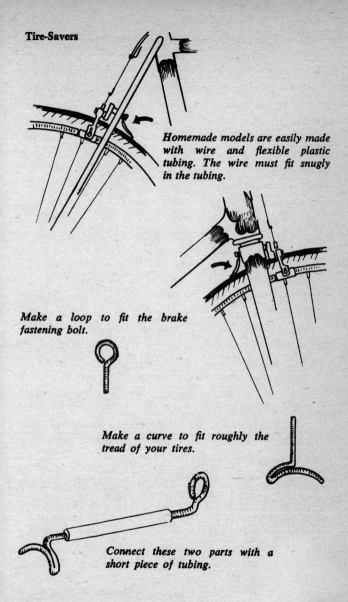

Homemade models are easily made with wire and flexible plastic tubing. The wire must fit snugly in the tubing.

Make a loop to fit the brake fastening bolt.

Make a curve to fit roughly the tread of your tires.

Connect these two parts with a short piece of tubing.

wood or cement tracks. Some ultralight road tires have this mat tread, too, but it is not satisfactory for touring or general traveling conditions. For one thing, wet conditions require some kind of tread to get through the moisture and make contact with the road. Many styles have been developed, but the most common now are the rib and a few types of mixed pattern. All of these styles can be found in tires, which range in weight from nine to fifteen ounces. The rib pattern is a marginally faster tread, whereas the mixed patterns are better suited to rougher conditions. I recommend a mixed tread for most touring and traveling, unless you anticipate consistently good roads.

It is possible, though unlikely, that you may need cyclo-cross tires. These have very heavy treads and often a larger cross section. Some, like the Clement 'Grifo,' have tractorlike lugs on the tread. They are originally intended for cyclo-cross racing, which is done on courses where at least half the race is on unpaved surfaces. This type of tire would be useful for muddy areas or dirt roads. As an exracer, I have a strong leaning towards light tires. However, I don't think it's wise to go under around ten ounces for touring purposes, especially if you are carrying luggage.

It's awfully difficult to recommend tire brand names. I've had bad luck with tires that others have been

Tread Patterns

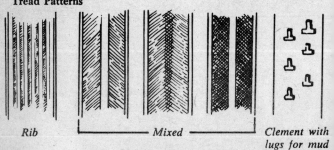

Rib   —————— Mixed ——————   Clement with
                                                lugs for mud

pleased with. Vittoria, for instance, are alleged to be *the* tire of European professional racers. But they've never lasted very well for me. First and secondhand observations lead me to use Pirelli cotton tires and the Clement range. Wolber has a good selection of medium and heavyweight tubulars that are pretty rugged. Makes like D'Allessandro, Canetti, Barum, Kondor, and La-Swiss are all good, but, I have too little firsthand experience with them to comment. On the negative side, Schwinn had, and may still have, a line of imported tubulars which were notorious for blowouts and other failures. Similarly, the Hutchinson tubulars, which come on the Peugeot 'PX-10,' are easily cut and prone to blowouts.

Tubular tire design is well suited to high pressures, but there are wired-on varieties which are made for high-pressure use, too. Although higher air pressure presents greater stress and increased chances of punctures and blowouts, tires made to take the stress have a couple of advantages. Lower rolling resistance is affected both by the firmer, less flexible quality of the tire and the amount of rubber in contact with the road is reduced. This latter factor emphasizes the importance of a good tread. A tire that is inflated hard is vastly more efficient than low-pressure varieties, but the road shock transmitted to the rider is increased. Thus, lower pressures, or a wider cross-sectional tire may be desirable for rough roads. Hard tires, bouncing on rough surfaces, not only increase your fatigue but reduce your efficiency and control since the wheels spend some of the time in the air. High-pressure wired-on tires made by such companies as Michelin, Clement, and Dunlop, can be pretty lightweight, especially when they are made with alloy rims. This combination can come close to the weight of the heavier ranges of tubulars. High-pressure wired-ons will take the pressure of eight to ninety pounds, where the regular

27 x 1¼ should be used at around seventy-five. Variations in pressure used depend on the weight of the rider. The weight of a heavier rider will flatten the tire more than a lighter one, so a little more pressure is necessary. Also, it is wise to reduce the pressure by a few pounds before a long ride on a hot day to compensate for the expansion that the heat can cause.

It is very important to keep a regular check on tire pressure, especially with tubulars which lose air quite rapidly. Low pressure puts the sidewalls through a lot of extra flexing and drastically increases the chances of the rim cuts that result when a bump pinches the tire between the rim and road. Tires just don't last very long without enough air. Further, underinflated tires can increase your energy output by as much as 30%. Obviously, too much air is also to be avoided. Many tires are exploded by people using air hoses at gas stations, which may be metered but are designed for car and truck tires and put a lot of air out fast. If you must use a gas station's hose, fill your tires a squirt at a time and check the pressure with a bicycle tire gauge or an educated thumb.

You probably won't blow out a tubular at a gas station. Pressures for tubulars depend on the same factors mentioned above, but at any rate never below 80 to 85 pounds. On smooth roads hard tubulars are a joy and are supremely efficient. You can use pressures up to 110 pounds with them. That sounds like a lot, but track riders sometimes go as high as 150.

There is no universal rule to help you decide what tires are good for what purposes. Some people use tubulars for long-distance touring with luggage; others find that to be expensive and inconvenient. If you are traveling light, with under twenty pounds of deadweight, tire mortality won't be unusually high, and you'll be spared the nuisance of fixing tires on the road. That means you get there a little less tired and/or go a little faster with tubulars. On the other hand, spare tires and tubes for the wired-on types are more universally available, and this is also true for spare rims should you damage the wheel. Sharp bumps with a lot of deadweight packed on the bike are more of a problem for tubular style rims than for the wired-on rims. If the route is going to be rocky or very rough, you are better off with wired-on. Under better conditions, when speed is a consideration, tubulars will do it better. But, differences in weight aren't as fundamental as your physical condition. Tubulars don't give you seven-league boots, they only help you make the best use of whatever shape you are in.

Folded Spare Tire

Pull the toe strap tight (or you'll lose it). Don't leave the tire folded in this manner for too long. Change to a spare and inflate the tire that was folded.

REPAIR

Besides lower weight, another advantage of the tubular tire to the racer is that it can be changed quickly and spares can be conveniently carried along. In fact, carry several for longer rides. This quality can also be important to the touring or camping rider who doesn't want to have to patch tires by the roadside. Since tubulars dispense with the stiff wires of conventional tires, they can be folded into a small bundle and tied with a toeclip strap behind the saddle or packed with the rest of the gear.

Changing the tire on the road can be accomplished in under five minutes. Simply pull the tire off the rim, starting opposite the valve. The glue should still be tacky enough for reuse unless it's old. Rolls of cotton tape, impregnated with rim cement, are convenient and clean to carry and apply. Tubes of glue have a habit of getting squashed, and tubular tire cement is the messiest, hardest to clean up stuff in the world. Use it at home, sparingly and not on the carpet. Getting back to your puncture, fit the replacement tire by starting with the valve in the valve hole. Then work the tire around the rim, stretching it on evenly and working away from the valve on both sides. Avoid getting glue on the sidewalls (or solvent for that matter, as it dissolves the rubber solution that keeps the threads together). You can tell if the tire is approximately centered by seeing if its base tape is in line with the edges of the rim. If the tire is new, especially with cheaper varieties, it may be a very tight fit and difficult to stretch onto the rim. Try stretching it a little first by hooking one end on your foot and pulling the other end. When you ride with tubulars, always carry a pump (or a valve adapter if you ride near gas stations) and a spare.

A puncture away from home with wired-on tires— always supposing you have a patch kit, tire irons, and pump—is usually a half-hour job to fix. A spare tube helps, but if the outer tire is shot you have to find alternate means of transport or a bike shop. But, since the wired-on is a sturdier tire, there is much less likelihood of having the puncture in the first place.

To fix it, lift the bead (wire) by inserting a tire iron underneath, prying it up, and hooking the other end of the lever on a spoke. Use a second tire iron to pry up the bead several inches to either side of the first and the tire should be loose enough to slide the lever all the way around. Then remove the tube and repeat the process with the other bead, which should be much easier. Fill the tube with air to find the leak, rub the area with fine sandpaper or the abrader that comes with most patch kits, apply rubber cement and let it dry completely. If you have to cut a patch from a larger piece, be sure to round the edge. Also make sure that the abraded and glued area is bigger than the whole patch. Square corners and unglued edges of patch can be the starting places from which the batch may be pulled off. Remove the backing of the patch and, without touching the face, press it firmly and squarely over the puncture.

The shape of the puncture can tell you something about how you got it. A simple tack or glass cut will appear as just a pinpoint hole or a slit. A blowout will cause a larger, ragged hole. A pair of little slits about an inch apart around the tube is characteristic of a rim cut, and both of these should be patched.

Before putting the whole thing back together, check the inside of the tire and the inside of the rim for whatever caused the puncture. If it is a long spoke end, it will have to be filed down. This is also a good time to check that the rim tape is in good enough condition to protect the tube from the spoke nipples. The debris in the tire that caused a puncture will probably still be there; so remove it. Don't use the tire irons to put the tire on again. Otherwise, the tube will get pinched between the iron and rim, and you may well puncture the tube again with a 'V' shaped wound. When refitting the tire, start the bead in the deepest part of the groove of the rim and you will find enough leeway to pull it on by hand. The fit will be tighter with high-pressure tires, but you still shouldn't need tire irons. Fit one side of the tire, then put enough air in the tube to give it shape, insert the valve in the rim and work the tube into the tire. Let the air out and fit the other side of the tire. When inflating the tire, the beads should press up to the shoulders of the rim. If some part of it doesn't, then some other section is going to ride too high, sometimes over the edge of the rim. In that case, deflate the tire, push the high spot down, and try to pull the low area up to start all over again. Sometimes it is necessary to remove the tire and reseat it.

The tubular tire, while convenient for fixing a puncture on the road, requires a more involved operation when it needs repairing because of the stitching. Patch kits are sometimes hard to find. Dunlop had a very fine one, but they are no longer being made. Velox is the only other brand that I've seen available here. I use a home-made patch kit. You need thin patches, which can be made from pieces of old tubular inner tube, rubber patching cement, a medium-sized sewing needle, and heavy linen thread or polyfilament high-test fishing line.

First find the puncture by filling the tire and sub-merging it in water. Air may travel inside the casing and escape around the valve although the actual puncture might be nowhere near it. When you find the puncture, air will be escaping from the casing in the area of the hole more than through the hole itself. Pull away the base tape a few inches to either side of the hole. This will reveal the stitching. In order to line up the sides for resewing after the patching, you should pencil a few reference marks across the stitched section. Pinch the sides of the tire together so that the stitches run along the edge. This will separate the stitching from the tube enough to make a cut without damaging the tube. Cut the stitches carefully down the middle and avoid cutting the casing. The incision need only be large enough to pull the tube out a few inches. Pull out the cut threads. Tweezers or pliers are very helpful in this operation. Most tires have a thin cotton tape lightly sewn just inside the

main stitching. If it is attached along both edges, this will have to be cut as well, but it doesn't need resewing.

Usually the puncture is apparent from visual inspection of the tube. If not, pump a little air into it and test it with your lips, making a saliva spot to mark it. The patching process is the same as for a tire but abrade the tube very lightly. Homemade patches should have solution applied to them as well as the tube. Small breaks in the casing can sometimes be fixed using a spare piece of casing applied to the inside with cement that is almost completely dry. Larger cuts are difficult to fix, considering their pressure-holding requirements. I use a patch of 'Mystic Tape' on the inside and then a wrap or two of Mystic Tape around the outside after sewing. Pinch the tire flat again and align the sewing holes by using the reference marks you made. Begin by sewing three to five stitches into the uncut threads and use a regular overhand stitch. Blowouts frequently occur when you begin the sewing where the old stitches left off or have not secured the end of the thread. Use the old sewing holes. Stitches should be firm but not so tight as to constrict the original dimension of the tire. Very tight sewing can damage the casing and is another source of blowouts. Loose sewing will produce a bulge. Then reattach the base tape with a half-dried coat of rubber cement. Mount the tire on the rim without glue for a couple of hours or overnight, partially inflated. The whole process can take as little as half an hour—with practice.

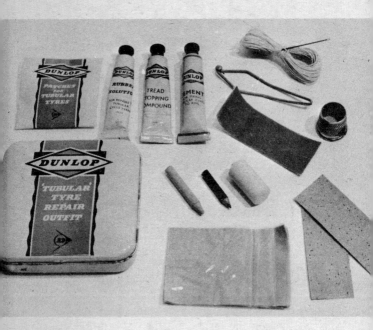

BRAKES

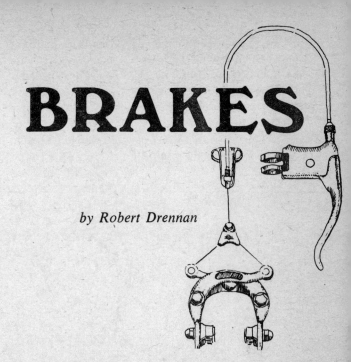

by Robert Drennan

The function of brakes found on ten-speed bicycles is extremely simple. They apply pressure to the rims of front and rear wheels, which slows and finally stops the bike. How they do that is very easy to understand and will be described. But perhaps more important when choosing a brake are the secondary factors concerning its functioning. Like any part of a bicycle, its weight and strength are important. But, the critical point is how reliable a brake's return action is, that is, how regularly and thoroughly a brake lets go of the rim when you want it to.

Though it may seem an ass-backwards way of approaching the subject, I'm going to give only a rudimentary description of how brakes stop bikes first and talk more about the fine points of their geometry and pad design much later. I think this is the way to come to the problem because this business of making sure your brakes don't hang up or rub while you're just pedaling along is very important. It is the issue that has the most far-reaching design implications. When you go to buy a new bike or replace the brakes that were originally on yours, picking those that won't hang up should be one of your three or four highest priorities.

Caliper or Side Pull Brake

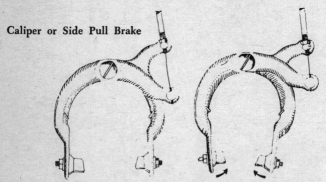

Bicycle brakes are little more than a pair of pivoted levers. One end of each lever is attached to a cable which, when pulled, rubs the other end of the levers against the wheel. Simple enough. The pad or rubbing end of the brake lever acts like the pads on a disc brake. This is a very efficient way of stopping a bike. There are a couple of ways of attaching cables to levers and a few more kinds and shapes of rubber that push against the rim, but basically, that's it.

Below there are illustrations of two kinds of bicycle brakes. They represent the two basic systems of pivoting their arms. The differences in their designs are not so significant in terms of stopping your bicycle. But the distinctions are very important in a number of other ways, most significantly in terms of the brake's letting go of the wheel and so not stopping it when you don't want it to.

In a caliper or side pull brake the cable is housed all the way down to the top attachment. The inner cable then extends to the lower arm and is attached to it. When you pull on the brake lever, the housing is driven downward and the cable is pulled up. The space between the two arms is contracted and both levers move, applying pressure to the rim.

On some side pull brakes, one arm may move farther than another because the housing may react differenly from the inner cable. This is compensated for once the first pad touches the rim of the wheel. It stays there, applying no additional pressure until the other side has swung into position. The two arms continue to so compensate and balance each other throughout the braking process.

The irregularities of this system have little or no effect on braking efficiency. But, there is a problem with the return action of the brakes. If a side pull goes in unevenly it will usually return unevenly and this can lead to one arm hanging up and rubbing on the rim after you've released the lever.

In a center pull the cable is the same, of course. However, the housing is mounted to the frame of the bike and the movement of the inner cable operates both arms. The inner cable is attached to the bowstring or

Center Pull Brake

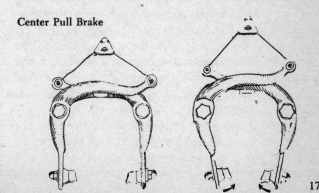

173

transverse cable across the top. It transfers pull to each brake arm and moves the pads against the rim. Occasionally, there is some uneven action in this transferal of pull to the two arms. However, the whole cable system is much more evenly balanced. The transverse cable hangs from the carrier and brake cable. The carrier is free to slide from side to side and so find the precise middle of the transverse cable. Thus, it centers itself and balances the force and travel of the brake arms.

The really important difference between these two types of brake is in their pivots. The side pull has only one and both arms turn on it.

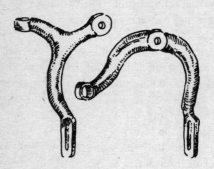

exploded view of side pull

As you can see, one arm rotates on the pivoting post in a clockwise direction and one in a counterclockwise direction. The post remains stationary as it is not only the pivot but also bolts the entire brake to the frame. In order to contract and return smoothly, a side pull must have high quality bearings isolating the opposing movements of the two arms. If it does not, the arms will work against each other, creating a stiffness.

There is another problem you may encounter. The pivot post on a side pull also attaches the brake to the frame. When you apply the brakes, the wheel rubs against the pads and tries to bend the whole brake backwards. So that it isn't successful in doing so, you have to bolt the brake firmly to the frame. This tightens the bearings of the pivot and the tighter they get the less effective they are in isolating the opposing movements of the arms. The tightened pivot and the pressure that the wheel puts on the brake while rubbing against it squeeze the bearings and cause friction between the arms.

The center pull, on the other hand, has two pivoting bolts, one for each arm.

A third, stationary part in a center pull, called a bridge, is bolted to the frame. At either end of the bridge there is a pivot for each arm of the brake. The effect of this arrangement is to separate all three functions—connecting the brake to the frame and pivoting both arms. Each of these three jobs is done at different points along the bridge.

The first nice effect of this arrangement is that you can bolt the center pull as securely as you'd like to the frame without having any effect on the pivot points of the arms. Tightening the frame connecting bolt only clamps the bridge down firmly. The pivoting relationship between the bridge and the arms is handled elsewhere.

A second and more important advantage of the

exploded view of center pull

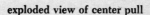
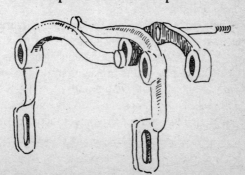

center pull is that the arm pivots don't work against each other. Bushings can be put on either side of each arm and the pivot bolts can be adjusted rather loosely so the whole thing works freely.

As I mentioned before, one of the greatest difficulties with brakes isn't getting them to stop bikes, it's getting the pads to let go of the wheel when you want them to. This is accomplished by a spring which applies an outward pressure on the brake. When you stop a bike by moving the arms into the rim, your hand is overcoming the force of this spring. When you let go, it should push the pads apart, away from the rim.

The complex single bearing mechanism and closer tolerances at the pivot of a side pull is difficult to overcome, especially for a spring that you have to be able to compress easily with the strength of your hand. The return action on a side pull is also more difficult because there can only be one spring bearing on its arms.

On a center pull each arm has a separate spring. Its bushings and looser pivots decrease return friction more effectively and so there is less of a tendency for the brake to hang up and rub the rim.

The trouble with many side pulls is that its single pivot is very complex. In order to operate properly and return fully, it has to be made in a very precise way. This doesn't mean you can't make a fine side pull brake. Campagnolo's brakes are side pulls and are considered by many to be the best in the world. But they cost as much as seventy dollars.

At any price level below that boggling figure, you're buying less than exquisitely manufactured brakes. As a result, the shortcomings of design in side pulls have a greater effect on ten dollar brakes than do the flaws that are going to show up in center pulls.

This discussion takes for granted that you're going to be able to find comparably manufactured, midprice range brakes of both types. The fact is that you won't be able to. Because there is a definite advantage to the center pull design, most manufacturers make their good brakes that way. The cheap junk brakes that they intend to sell to Americans are of the side pull variety. The effect is that most side pull brakes are either very good or very bad. They simply can't be adequate if they are tooled to a moderate price range. Chances are you're not in the market for the very good ones.

When you buy a brake you generally get a lever with it. It is almost always comparable in design and manufacture to the brakes themselves and so you can decide on a brake assembly by choosing a good brake. However, there are a few details to consider at this end of your stopper that may affect what brake you use.

One important position in the tourist's riding style is to lean the heel of the thumb on the brake lever. As a result, this part should be wide enough not to dig into your hand. An added plus are those levers which are rubber hooded and so cushion your grip even more.

The shape of the lever should conform to the shape of your bars so that they are easy to get at when you're riding. The configuration of most levers is pretty much the same and unless you buy some really odd or ill-suited brake assembly, this shouldn't be a problem. It is worth thinking about in attaching your levers. Some tourists enjoy the riding position that rests the heels of the thumbs on the brakes so much that they move the levers high on the bars to make this a more erect position. The net effect is to make braking from down positions very difficult. Remember, the contour of the forward, down-turning part of the bar should conform to the brake lever. The lever should be accessible from any hand position and conveniently placed so, if you have to, you can stop hard.

Cables stretch, especially on a long tour. It isn't

difficult to adjust the cables on any brake. All you have to do is get off, loosen a nut or two and tighten them. With a heavy load of gear and constant riding, however, it's nice to be able to keep your cables adjusted all the time. With lever-mounted cable adjusters you can do this as you ride. These are convenient extras that are good safety devices if you are slow to adjust brakes that need it. The things that are easy to do are more likely to get done most often.

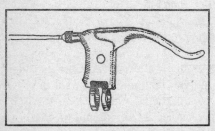

Finally, brake levers are big and so should be as light as possible. Brake levers made of alloys are best. Mafac, which makes pretty good brakes, makes steel levers; so, if you can, replace them.

Adjusting your cables is a serious business in a lot of ways. Most important of these is that you ride so that the pads are as close to the rim as possible. This gives you a fistfull of brake. In other words, when you apply the lever there is very little travel to it before the pads hit the wheel. The remaining travel is all brake, various degrees of pressure, and stopping power. This travel before the pads hit the rim should be no more than 25% of the levers' arc.

Of course, if your brake pads are going to be very close to the rim, the wheels of your bicycle have to be true enough so that bends in them don't rub against the pads. Perhaps more difficult is removing the wheel to repair a flat tire. The diameter of the tire is greater than that of the rim. If the pads pinch in close to the rim, you won't be able to get the tire off easily or quickly. Hence, the 'quick-release.'

The quick-release device is either at the hanger above the brake on a center pull or on the lever. It is a cam or spacer that allows you to slacken the cable and expand the brakes so that you can get the tire off. If you are going to do serious touring, a quick-release mechanism of some kind is as important as a patch kit.

The relatively simple device of the cable comes into any discussion of brakes many times. Cables stretch and so have to be adjusted. There is one other important factor about them: The metal inner cable will rub on its housing when you operate the brake. In fact, most of the friction in a breaking system is in that cable. So that the brakes will return properly, you should clean and lubricate your cables before any long ride. This is easy: All you have to do is pull the inner cable out and clean it, spray an aerosol lubricant like motorcycle chain oiler into the housing and then coat the inner cable with 'Lubriplate' grease.

This simple maintenance operation will improve your touring. In fact, the problem with the long housings and excessive friction involved in rear brakes has lead some manufacturers to try and eliminate much of this housing. They braze lugs beneath the top tube and run the inner cable exposed. This cuts out a lot of housing and thus also friction, but you can accomplish the same end with careful lubrication.

BRAKES

There are very few high quality brakes made. Those that are discussed here are among the best or most popular or both. They are all made of alloy of one kind or another and, with the exception of the last two, are all center pulls. They work well and are reliable. Some, however, are much more simply designed and built than others. In order for a bicycle to be reliable to an extreme, simplicity should be the essence of its construction. They should be, basically, stark and well-honed minimums and any touchy extras only add to the chances of failure. If you're going to tour, look at everything you plan to use and decide if your bike is simply and sturdily built. Beyond all the sophistications of design and manufacture, this basic simplicity will contribute most to long and maintenance free mileage.

GB

These are English brakes and (though I betray my prejudice) are made like most British machines with odd and overly complicated details. The quick-release function is found at the lever and is a plastic spacer that is

operated with a fragile spring. It works but is potentially a weak point.

GB chooses to hang the pivots of both arms from posts that are very securely mounted. They are supported on both sides by a kind of frame that either indicates a distrust of their own abilities or an attempt at a unique and useful design. Perhaps both. Anyway, the arms operate well enough and return adequately but this brake simply doesn't distinguish itself.

GB brakes are hard to find and don't come as standard equipment on many bikes, but they're out there if you want to look for them.

Mafac

Mafac is a French firm. They make three brakes that are all the same size and price but that have some differences. Generally, Mafac's forte is adjustability. They go to considerable lengths to see that the pads of their brakes will apply pressure in an optimal way to the rim.

The Mafac 'Racer' costs seven dollars. Its most notable characteristic is its multiple adjustable pads.

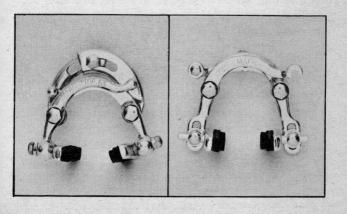

Whereas most brakes have slots that will allow for adjusting the pads up and down, the Mafac also allows you to move them in and out and aim them at the rim. This system is very well-regarded by some bikers. I've found almost all the brakes costing about seven dollars fit very well without this extra capability. The Mafac design sacrifices more positive pad shaft support for mobility and, to me, it isn't worth it.

Mafac makes their brakes out of 'Dural' aluminum, a very light and strong material that finishes very well.

The only other unusual detail in design of note on the Mafac is the bolt that connects the bridge to the frame. It isn't keyed. That is, the bridge can rotate slightly. This isn't a big problem because you can tighten the bolt as much as you'd like without affecting the action of the brake. However, a keyed and so immobile bridge would be better.

Mafac also makes the 'Top 63', a superadjustable brake. It is identical to the 'Racer' in every way except the bridge is a sliding, two piece, adjustable affair. The overkill of the adjustable pads is only aggravated by this really unusual design. Doing your own work on these brakes is harder than on others and the bridge isn't as rigid as it might be. If you find you have a strange bike with odd wheels, this brake may help, but I have never seen such a machine and can't imagine it.

Weinmann

Weinmann makes really excellent brakes. The 'Vainqueur' series is a simple and lightweight brakes that is relatively inexpensive ($6.90) and very reliable.

These brakes come in two arm lengths. Being able to fit the shorter of the two styles to your machine is a decided advantage. Simply enough, the smaller the pad arm as measured from the pivot, relative to the length of the cable end of the arm, the greater mechanical ad-

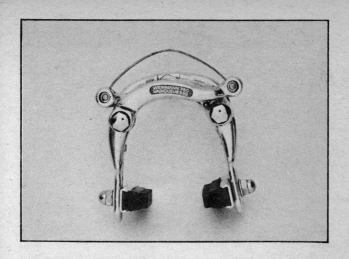

vantage at the pad. This makes it possible to apply terrific force to the rim when you need to stop in a hurry or when you are carrying a load. This arm-length option is available on a number of brakes and you should take advantage of it if possible.

The only thing that might limit your using this shorter armed model is the rim and tire you have on your bike. Generally, wired on tires are larger than tubulars and so you have to fit larger brakes to accommodate the larger tires. If you've got tubulars, try to use the smaller brakes as they'll stop you faster.

Wienmann's brakes come with an unusual keying device between the two arms. This forces them to operate simultaneously and always to the same degree. If the bearings at either of the arms should be fouled with road dirt, this key will force the return of both arms and so further insure against the brake hanging up.

The quick-release function on a Weinmann brake is excellent and works well. They are light, effective, and reliable components. In the moderate price range you can hardly do better. Some riders prefer the Universal '61' to Weinmann's equipment, but this is by no means beyond argument. The Universal costs $12.95, about twice the price of the Weinmann.

Universal

Universal's top center pull is called the '61'. It comes as standard equipment on the Fregus, Legnano, and Bottechia professional models and so is clearly a very highly regarded stopper. It's beautifully designed and simple. In fact, there's nothing about it that can be reasonably criticized. It works well and is very strong.

Universal's seven dollar brake is also very good. It is made in the same design as the '61' and has a number of its simple and effective characteristics. For an inexpensive brake it has good bearings and so operates smoothly.

There are two makers of really good side pulls. Universal is one of them. Their '51' and '68' are very finely made and reliable brakes that overcome the limitations of the complex pivot of a caliper brake. These both cost between fifteen and seventeen dollars. The Universal '68' is the top of this excellent line and works like a dream.

I think the quality increase per dollar that is

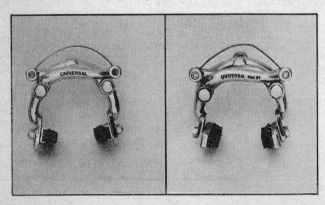

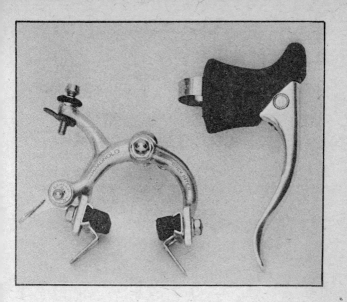

achieved by buying a '68' makes these brakes worth the
money. They are not only functionally flawless, but they
are very attractive as well.

The only brake that surpasses these are Campagnolo's 'Record' caliper brakes. Campagnolo's are almost
certainly no more reliable or effective than good Univer-
sals or Weinmanns but they are so superbly made that
they remain the choice on the very finest bicycles. They
are very expensive, fifty-five to seventy dollars and only
worth the money if you have the bug in the worst way
possible. At least go to a shop and handle these brakes
in order to appreciate the state of their art. As for their
appearance, let me only say that I apologize for the less
than ideal paper on which we are reproducing these pictures. The real thing is extraordinary. ●

CAMPING

TENTS

by James Fuller

Survival manuals and woodslore how-to books are marvels of ingenuity. Almost any handbook will illustrate shelters made from tarps or ponchos that involve any number of lopped and bent trees, lashed boughs, and improvised stakes. Many campers still use these techniques but their effect on the environment is considerable. Backpacking and camping in general have become increasingly popular and the growing traffic over limited open lands has only been aggravated by this kind of misuse. Cheap, effective, self-contained shelters that put an end to 'make-do' and vicarious survival techniques are easily available, so use them.

Modern lightweight and durable materials have

been applied to the business of making backpacking and mountaineering tents. The result is a wide variety of compact, lightweight equipment that is surprisingly spacious when in use. But, just as technology has applied itself to materials, so it has specialized design. Many modern tents are designed and built for extreme conditions and are not only much more expensive than needed but aren't as comfortable for the moderate conditions of two wheel camping.

The high altitude mountaineer, camping above timberline, plans to spend little time in his tent. It should be very small for added warmth and must be extremely light. Because of the high winds and snow that mountaineers run into, their tents must be rugged, with heavy gauge poles and hardware, and made entirely of sturdy fabrics. The low profiles of mountain tents minimize the chance of hundred-mile-per-hour winds blowing the whole thing over. Sleeve tunnel entrances and provisions for cooking inside are common as well because campfires aren't cozy at high altitudes.

Lots of this is expensive and most of it will never be needed by the cyclist. Though high quality construction is always a plus and durability is a big factor, really high winds and drifting snow aren't a real problem for the tourist. He has to worry more about rain and bugs, can be less concerned about how tough a tent is, and so think about its weight and versatility. Poles, pegs, guy lines, and even fabrics need not be so strong and can, therefore, be lighter and cheaper.

Of course, there are decisions to make when conditions make different shelters possible. A cyclist can opt for a really large two-or three-man tent and still carry very little weight. Or, because he can pick his climate, he may well decide on a small, simple tent that he'll use only for getting out of the rain. The least sophisticated of shelters, like rain flies or ponchos can be relied on and set up in a number of ways. Finally, you can sleep without shelter at all. This last possibility is really best in much of the United States.

The arguments for carrying a tent are simple: There's no better way to beat the rain, the wind or the bugs. Also, in crowded, close-plot camping facilities privacy is a consideration.

The best argument against tents comes to me from Colin Fletcher, who walks to where privacy isn't a problem. Tents, along with cameras and campfires, cut him off, cut him off the way megaphones on a British twin cut me off. They do to him what an empty six-pack does to a field.

For rain, there are a number of less-than-tent-roofs that can be put to good service. They're cheap, some very cheap, and if you use them right, they work well. But before making a decision on what to choose, consider the functions a tent is designed to fulfill, then decide which you expect of your shelter.

One way or another you've got to carry your tent around. The recurring problem of weight and bulk rules out really large, family type, canvas tents. The problem is getting as much adequately sheltered internal space as possible when the tent is in use, for a minimum of weight and packed bulk when it is not. Nylon is considerably stronger than cotton, and so tents of equal or greater durability can be made using less material. Thus, they are not only less bulky but are much lighter as well.

Cotton's shortcomings aren't limited to its massiveness. Condensation will be discussed later, but another water problem is the capillary leakage of single-walled cotton tents. Touch the wall when it is wet and it leaks. This is a big disadvantage especially when, in order to limit the load you're carrying, the tent has been designed as a small shelter rather than a large living area.

You should be able to bang around and pack gear against the walls of a small tent, but in a cotton one you can't.

Motorcyclists aren't so certainly limited to nylon as are bicyclists, and because cost differences are great between the two they may well be the only practical alternative. Good cotton tents can be bought from most general camping suppliers, but mountain and backpacking specialists usually don't carry them.

Other than design differences applicable to most tents, the sort of cotton used is the most important criteria for judging the quality of the tent.

Generally, 'Army Duck' is the best. It has a high thread count per square inch (i.e., is closely woven), is dry-finished, and has some breatheability. Army Duck is the best of the 'drill' type fabrics. When produced for use in tents thread counts in drills run to four hundred or more which makes for a durable and water tight tent. Other acceptable, if heavy materials run in weight from six to eight ounces per yard and have thread counts ranging from 125-200 per square inch.

In deciding among the many fabrics available, it's best to avoid 'filler' used in manufacture. These treated materials clog up any pores that might breathe moisture out of the tent. High thread counts and low weight are the factors to look for and are usually found among combed poplins and good drill materials. One other thing: Almost everyone manufacturing tent material treats cotton for mildew. Trust the effect of this treatment very little and don't pack tents when they're damp.

One of the best things a tent does is keep the bugs out. There are some good insect repellants on the market, some, even, that repel bugs, but it's better to put a screen between you and them. It's even fun, in an odd moment, to watch them try to get through. Good tents have nylon netting sewn into vents and windows and positive zip

191

closings on doorways. In fact, look for tight, secure closures on doors and flaps too.

The whole business of seams and flaps is an important one. A healthy amount of overlap and closely sewn seams makes for a stronger and tighter seal. Where cotton threads are used there is less chance of leakage because the cotton swells when wet, but any other type of thread, though perhaps stronger, should be sealed with some sort of cement.

Seams are a relatively minor issue in dealing with the only three-season problem that has precedence over bugs: the rain. It happens that the worst of it is not just keeping the water out.

When you sleep in a tent your body warms the inside and a full pint of insensible perspiration may evaporate into this warmed air during a night. When it rains, airborne water vapor is absorbed by the warmer air in the tent and increases even more the concentration of moisture.

The plastic coating that makes nylon water repellant holds water in as well as out, and so water vapor remains inside. Though a single layer tent may shed the water that falls on it, the rain's cooling effect lowers the temperature of the tent shell to the point where water suspended inside condenses on the walls and roof. So much water can accumulate in there where you live that it's worse than no tent at all.

A single wall cotton tent needs little or no waterproofing because the cotton swells when wet. However, as the pores of the cotton close it reacts to vapor in the same way as coated nylon: neither can breathe and exhale the humid air inside and so it condenses. Any single layer tent that's coated or naturally impervious to water will have condensation problems. Manufacturers periodically announce the development of waterproofing materials that can breathe, but they are inevitably compromises, neither holding out all the rain nor allowing most of the interior vapor to escape. Lots of people get along pretty well with these tents, but don't expect them to do what they say they do.

Even when good ventilation is possible, condensation occurs, and usually the need for moving air through the tent is greatest when the rain prohibits opening vents and doors.

The solution is a tent designed to use a fly-sheet. Double walled tents, though heavier and more bulky, work well.

A fly-sheet is a tent over the tent, separated from the inside walls and roof by an air space of about four inches. The fly is made of waterproof, plastic-coated nylon that protects you from the rain.

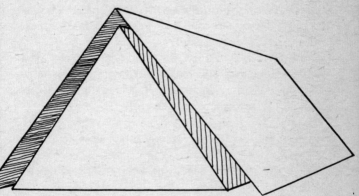

With a fly the inner tent can be ventilated in two ways. The most obvious is to open the windows. More importantly, the inside tent can be made of woven, highly porous, and breatheable taffeta or ripstop nylon. This untreated, water permeable material allows vapor to pass through it, condense on the fly, and soak the ground outside the inner tent or be evaporated into the air-space. In addition, this material is more readily warmed

193

above the dew point and so does not condense vapor.

Double-walled backpacking tents with fitted fly-sheets are costly. You can buy untreated cotton or nylon tents without flys (which alone can run to $40) and fit over the tent a cheap, expendable plastic sheet with grommets or Visklamps. If water stays off, the cotton won't swell and so will remain breatheable. However, this system will not work as well as a good, all nylon, double-walled tent.

The advantages of this system are considerable even beyond the condensation problem. The inner tent can be made of very durable material while the less expensive, replaceable fly can be nylon too loosely woven to be waterproof once the coating has cracked through long use.

The fly, if tightly drawn and pitched close to the inner tent, is good winter insulation. In the summer it reflects the sun's heat and keeps the inside cooler.

In spite of manufacturing techniques designed to improve seams, they still leak. Two layers of tent eliminate the difficulty. The same, of course, applies to less than perfect repair jobs.

Because there is no floor sewn into the fly, runoff water is still a problem. Nearly all modern tents have waterproof floors and coating ten inches or more on the sidewalls. The best system is the 'bathtub' floor which is a

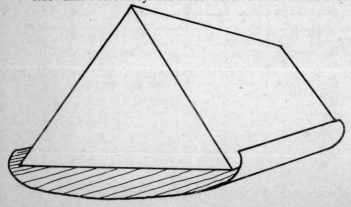

single piece of coated nylon which runs several inches up the sidewall so that there is no chance of seam leakage at ground level. The roof is left uncoated.

Tents come with lots of optional extra niceties. Many come with shock cords that hold collapsible poles together in your pack. You can get models with tabs on the sidewalls that guy the wall of the tent outward, increasing the internal volume of the standard 'A' frame shape. Either this, eight feet of length or a built in vestibule is a good idea if you expect to store gear inside. Some come with pockets inside and coat hanger loops and I once saw an ashtray clamped to a collapsible pole.

Color is a little more important than you'd imagine. Hot, violent colors are irritating if you have to stay in there too long. Softer colors, like tan, burnt orange, or yellow, make for a more pleasant interior. Bright international orange, however, can be seen best by hunters and is safer if you're off the road when anything that moves is in season.

The function of a tent is to control the environment within it. It not only excludes rain, wind and insects but also retains warmth. Other than considerations of cost, and the relative problems of weight and bulk, there are a few basic functions that you should check for in any tent.

It should keep out the rain and ground water. Waterproof floors and sidewalls and ideally a single-piece bathtub floor protect from ground leakage. A fly-sheet is a necessary item if you really want to stay dry even in prolonged rain.

Positive closure on netting and on flaps and doors as well will keep insects out.

Plan how much space you're going to need, not only for the people but for their gear, too. Dunnage, especially when unpacked, can be bulky, so leave some room for it.

Before you decide if you need a tent find out what non-tent-roofs can do. Many simple, adaptable forms of shelter can be improvised and require even less weight and bulk than complete tents. However, they sacrifice one or more of the uses that tents fulfill. (A short discussion of some of their forms follows this section on tents.)

Finally, be careful where you pitch a tent. In spite of their comforts, moss and soft tundra are extremely fragile biospheres that can not rebound from hard use. Though most state and national parks have small, clearly marked sites for camping, some do not. Where you are left to camp more freely make the most of the fact that your shelter needn't take the place you're living in, scarf it up, and dump on it.

TENTS

Bishop's Pack-Lite and Camp-Rite Tents

The makers of Bishop's 'Ultimate Tents' offer these two man models and, like their larger tents, they are excellent. Designed and priced for the serious backpacker, the 'Pack-Lite' is both compact and very light weight. The 'Camp-Rite' is cotton and can be had without the fitted fly-sheet in order to save some money. A cheaper, plastic flat fly can then be improvised.

Robert Blanchard invented the 'Draw-Tite' tent, a system that is now copied by a number of manufacturers. The basis of the system is a very strong, heat treated, aluminum alloy frame which is rigidly tensioned and erected outside the tent. The shell is then strung inside the frame and fastened tightly to it. The high altitude advantage of this system is that it reduces high wind flapping and sagging. For the tourist, it offers considerably more room inside.

Barry Bishop, who made the summit of Everest, and Robert Blanchard are uncompromising tent manufacturers. Their tents include such conveniences as full doors and screens at either end, external frame design, and bath tub type floors which extend up the sidewalls before they are sewn to the main walls. This minimizes the chance of groundwater leakage at a seam. With their optional cotton liners, both the Camp-Lite and Camp-Rite can be used in snow.

The Bishop handout pamphlet is very informative. It has lines in it such as: "It was early decided that commercial considerations would *not* be a factor. In this no compromise tent, cost would not be a consideration; hence the name 'Ultimate'." And this one about the largest mountain tents: "Your Sherpas can put this tent up in the dark without making the campground look like a Chinese fire drill."

Bishop's Ultimate Outdoor Equipment
6804 Millwood Road
Bethesda, Maryland 20034

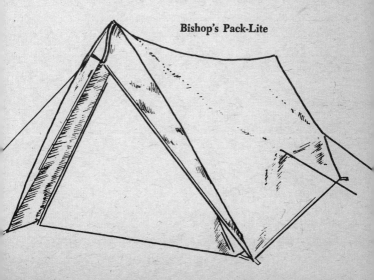

Bishop's Pack-Lite

Blacks

Blacks began manufacturing tents in Britain in 1905 and remain the best known supplier there. They now have mail order and retail facilities in Canada and Ogdensburg, New York.

The majority of their tents are still the old style, made of Egyptian cotton and are too heavy for backpacking. They now make a few lightweight nylon models. Blacks' standard line is designed around a center pole so the optional angle poles, which are set up outside the tent, should be ordered. These poles cost very little extra. The tents also come without rear windows and should have one added at $9.50 extra.

The best thing about them is that they are rugged.

Thomas Black and Sons, Ltd.
225 Strathcona Avenue,
Ottawa 1, Ontario, Canada

Thomas Black and Sons, Inc.
930 Ford Street,
Ogdensburg, New York   13669

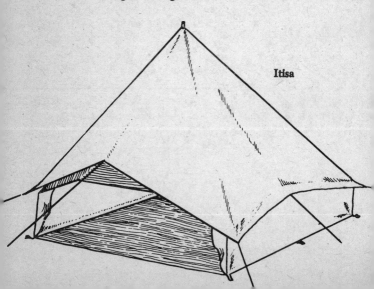

Itisa

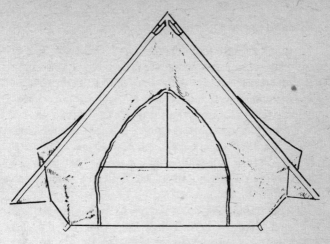

Sierra Designs' Hexagonal

Sierra Designs

Sierra Designs makes large, high quality mountain tents and their craftsmanship and materials are all the best. Generally, however, these are specialized to an extreme. They have cookholes and tunnel entrances which are expensive and are certainly unnecessary for the biker.

The hexagonal three-man is probably their only tent really suited to the needs of the motorcyclist or bicyclist. It's very big, with enough room for two and plenty of gear. This tent has three external poles, a zipper in the fly-sheet for easy access to the door and two really large screened vents. Getting the six-sided floor just so is a nuisance, but the whole thing is very stable once you've got it set up.

Sierra Designs
4th and Addison Streets
Berkeley, California 94710

Eureka Tent and Awning Company

Eureka's full line is dominated by large, family tents that weigh a ton and house armies of station-wagon vacationers. Those in their line that suit the cyclist are reasonably well made and, in light of their back-packing features, are very inexpensive. Eureka makes some pretty good tents that aren't listed in the table. Their 'Mark II,' 'Mark IV,' and 'Two-Man High Lite' are all good, double-walled, nylon tents. They're in the higher price ranges, however, and better equipment can be had for the money.

The 'mountain' tents come in two-, three-, and four-man sizes. They're a little heavy for the bicyclist but have nice features like screens at the doors with three-way zippers. The door has a single vertical zipper and the single pull outs make them much more roomy. Too bad there aren't two or three of them.

The 'Mount Marcy' is an economy tent, with room for two and gear, that's very light. It's made of high quality ripstop nylon. It's the lowest priced, really lightweight tent I know. The failing of the tent is its single-walled design. Condensation is a problem when the vents must be closed. However, there are not only large screened doors at one end and a screened window in the rear but long side windows as well. With an oversized, inexpensive plastic fly extending over the front and rear, circulation can be maintained and some of the condensation curbed. But really prolonged rain will make it wet inside.

The 'Mount Katahdin' is a breatheable version with the fly-sheet of the Mount Marcy. Equally roomy and well made, the tent proper is uncoated nylon, while the flat, extended fly is coated. The distinction will cost you $20.00 and is worth it if you've got it. The Katahdin is blue, which is easier on the occupants' eyes than the Marcy's orange.

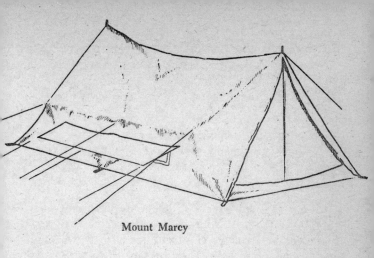

Mount Marcy

Alpine Draw-Tite Tents

This is a very popular design, for reasons that escape me. It's not cheap, but it's roomy, has no interior poles because of the unique 'Blanchard' type frame and is heavy. Eastern Mountain Sports carries a nylon version with a full fly-sheet. This nylon model weighs only 8 pounds 4 ounces, but runs a handsome $140.00. Eureka only markets the 6.5 ounce poplin version with a top or cap fly, which is less than perfect.

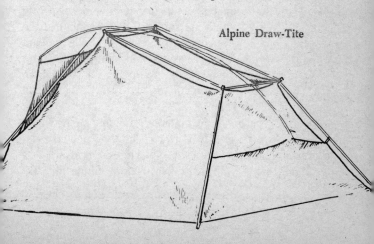

Alpine Draw-Tite

There are some nicer things to say about these tents. They need no pegs and can be picked up and moved in tact once set up.

For information on Eureka's tents write to:

Eureka Tent and Awning
625 Conklin Road
Bingham, New York   13902

Gerry

Gerry's innovations in design are intelligent, effective and carried off with fine workmanship. They result in a good, extremely lightweight line of tents, which are extraordinarily roomy. They are tapered to save weight and the larger, center peek tents have room for you to stand at their center. Detail like nylon zippers and large, taut fly-sheets make them convenient and effective protection.

The 'Lodgepole' and 'Fireside' tents are inexpensive only in relation to their quality. They have features and craftsmanship similar to the more expensive tents in the Gerry line but are designed for more moderate conditions, that is, any the summer cyclist is likely to run into.

Both the Lodgepole and Fireside have permanently attached fly-sheets that are sewn to the inner tent at the ridgeline and connected with shock cords to the walls at ground level. This unusual fly and tent combination is very easy to pitch. They are higher in front than rear, but are roomy enough for two. They are also an easy to live with green.

The 'Yearound' two-man is a more sophisticated tent. It has a flattened 'A' frame and external pole design which increases the usable interior space. It also has a mountain type, thirty-six inch front vestibule for gear storage. This is about as good a two-man as you'll find,

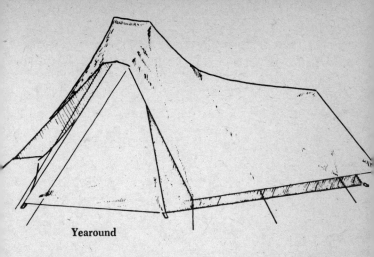

Yearound

the distinctions beyond this quality of tent are matters of personal preference. Except in winter or driving rain the Lodgepole will serve as well and for less money.

> Gerry
> 5450 North Valley Highway,
> Denver, Colorado   80216

Alpine Designs

Alp equipment has had considerable success and their operations have grown with the boom in camping sales. Their tents are well thought out examples of lightweight shelter, using nylon zippers, dacron-cotton thread to prevent seam leakage, polyurethane-coated flies and waterproof floors and sidewalls.

The 'Yosemite' line is the most interesting. This patent pending design involves a center external 'A' frame that supports the coated fly rather than the tent proper. The inner tent is a loose weave cotton-polyester that is permanently attached to the fly with nylon netting, and hangs inside almost Blanchard-style. That portion of the fly which overhangs the inner shelter produces a

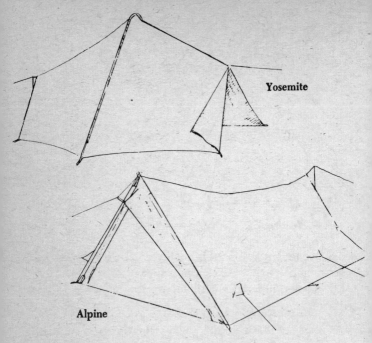

Yosemite

Alpine

large, floorless front vestibule. Both the two- and three-man are two-man tents with relatively more or less elbow room.

The 'Alpine' and 'Timberline' tents are also good. The Alpine is equipped with niceties like clothes loops at the ridgeline seam and two pockets sewn into the inside walls for eyeglasses and the like. The Alpine is the only Alp tent that comes with pegs.

Alpine Designs does not have mail order facilities for direct sale to the consumer, but many retailers handle their equipment. Write for their catalogue. It has good photos and is in color.

Alpine Designs
6185 East Arapahoe Street
Box 3561
Boulder, Colorado   80303

Warmlite Tents

Warmlite produces extremely lightweight tents, which are, like their sleeping bags, coated. They rely on a rubber urethane coating over 1.2 ounce ripstop nylon for water repellancy and yet breathing qualities as well. Options on the tents include a number of large windows and a moisture absorbent liner. Never having used the tent I don't know if the single-walled, coated nylon really breathes. The catalogue testimonials say it does.

Warmlite produces a unique 'filmgap' liner that goes inside their 'Model 7' tents and, reportedly, eliminates the need for sleeping bags. The liner, however, is a complex, ten layer lamination and runs a healthy $200.00.

These tents are fantastically light and compact relative to their sizes when pitched.

For Warmlite's catalogue, which is interesting in itself, write to:

Stephenson's
23206 Hatteras Street
Woodland Hills, California   91364

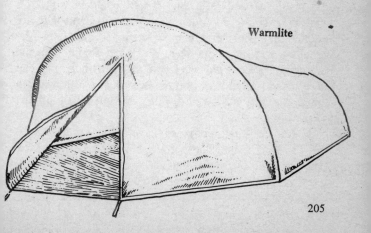

Warmlite

LESS-THAN-TENT-ROOFS

Touring and camping in summer, especially in areas where you can expect little rain, allows you to make plans to use shelters only occasionally. Less than thorough, even makeshift protection is enough when conditions are mild, and when they're not, minimal shelter is effective if well thought-out. A canopy that has walls and a roof but no floor isn't a tent. But though they are little more than bivouacs and have less than sophisticated designs doesn't mean these roofs shouldn't be considered as possible shelters for the biker.

Sleeping in the rain, on a picnic table, with a poncho guyed over your bag, may make you feel like you're hiding from the weather. But, so long as it works, and you're not discovered, the shelter's served its purpose.

Foremost among the bivouac's strengths is its very low cost. Even the simplest of them will keep the rain off nearly as well as a tent (better than one without a rain-fly if you've a condensation problem) and they are lighter and considerably more compact than even the smallest mountain equipment. For most summer bikers, wind and severe cold are not a problem, but a fly can be pitched so that it will retain more than a little warmth on cold nights. As awnings, they will effectively protect you from the sun.

But less-than-tent-roofs have their failings. Like the pup tent, they do little if anything by way of protecting you from bugs, and unless they're carefully pitched, they will leak ground water. Of course, a bivouac isn't the most private of places, but a large one can be folded and tied to be pretty well sealed off from your campground neighbors.

The bivouac's major advantage over the tent is its versatility. If it's equipped with a number of grommets and tabs and you've brought poles, guys, and stakes, you can shape it to fit the particular conditions of your camp site. But don't plan on pitching it with what's around. Rocks and trees are unreliable stakes and poles, so don't count on them. Carry poles especially so that in order to get out of the rain, you won't have to cut and bend the trees around your site.

Even if you go equipped with a tent, provisions for a simple bivouac can be an effective way of protecting your gear and bike. Similarly, because a fly can be so quickly and easily erected, you can temporarily set it up to sit out a shower.

There is little to be said concerning these simple shelters beyond a brief run down of the equipment that is available. However, one general point may help. Woodsmen have long erected high peaked lean-to's and wall tents of all kinds, and many manuals outlining techniques for building them can still be bought in book stores. One of the advantages of strung-together shelters made of flat, waterproof sheets is the savings in weight they offer. So, if you plan on this type of protection, plan also to pitch it low and wide. Not only will the roof be more stable, but it will cover the greatest amount of stuff with the least amount of tenting material in this way. Be careful to pitch the roof enough so that it will shed rain, however, or it will collect puddles and eventually leak.

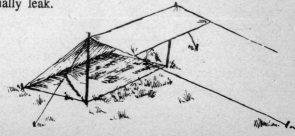

The Fly-Sheet

Probably the most common bivouac is a large nylon sheet much like the flat flies used in double-walled tents. These can be bought with any number of grommet and tab variations sewn into them or can easily be made from retailers' fabric stocks of either coated or uncoated ripstop nylon. If you're making your own, coated nylon is, of course, more waterproof, but the less expensive uncoated material is adequate except in a really driving rain. Because the fly cannot help but be relatively light, use a heavy weight nylon of at least three ounces in order to make it more durable. Because it will be pretty cheap to buy, make it extra large, for instance, nine by sixteen feet.

There are also a few touches that you can either work into a homemade fly or add to one you buy that will contribute considerably to the ease with which it can be pitched. The ridge will make a more symmetrical shelter and the poles will be more secure if you've sewn grommets into the edge of the fly which will just fit over the tapered top of your poles but will not slide down their length. Similarly, 'D' rings or tapes sewn into the edges will make guying simpler.

Store-bought ground sheets and flies are available in urethane coated nylon known as 'Nylport,' which is the best of the suitable light weight materials. Most major retailers sell them, but, as an example, one sold by Holubar has grommets in all four corners and seventeen additional ties on the edges and on the body of the tarp. It measures 7' x 10', weighs twenty-five ounces, and costs $27.00. Coated nylon sheets that are not Nylport and thus are not as durable are considerably less expensive. From Recreational Equipment, Inc. you can get 7' x 9', twenty-four ounces and only $10.95. The fabric for a home-made Nylport fly measuring about

7' x 10' costs about $14.00. Suppliers for the material to put your own together are listed in the article on "Making Your Own."

For the motorcyclist, if not for the more weight conscious bicyclist, poplin dining flies sold by a number of general camping equipment retailers are a possibility. Their intended purpose is as a sort of patio off of a large family wall tent. These flies, because they're usually used by station-wagon campers, are neither cheap nor light. But they're very strong. Though there are many, Eureka is among the largest suppliers of these dining flies.

7 x 9	$ 8.50
8 x 10	10.50
10 x 12	15.50
12 x 14	22.25
12 x 18	28.50

From Eureka, also, come some of the least expensive coated ripstop nylon flies. These are extremely lightweight, only 1.1 ounce per yard, and must be treated with some care.

6 x 8	$ 8.95
9 x 10	14.25
10 x 12	18.95

White 'Visqueen' polyethylene sheets are extremely inexpensive flies. These are completely waterproof, plastic sheets that are surprisingly rugged for their .004 inch thickness. Ragtag shelters that are often 50% folds and that change with the wind or the whim of their owner can be made from these sheets. But, they must be treated carefully. Ideally, reinforcement by way of a cloth adhesive of some kind should be added because this material is even more fragile than the lightest weight nylon. However, because this precaution isn't likely to be followed, it's just as easy to carry a spare since the stuff is so light and inexpensive. A sample list, from Recreational Equipment, Inc. reads as follows:

6 x 8	1	pound	$ 1.00
8 x 9	1½		1.49
9 x 12	2		2.10
12 x 12	3		2.95
24 x 24	11½		10.95

Cloth adhesive for reinforcing poly-tarps comes in thirty-six-foot rolls from Recreational Equipment for 98¢.

One likeable compromise in tarps or flys is the 'Versa Tarp.' It is a plastic sheet reinforced throughout with nylon and so is 'tear resistant' or at least tougher than plastic sheeting. Eastern Mountain Sports sells it with twelve 'Versa Ties,' devices for attaching guy lines to the tarp. An 8′ x 6′ sheet costs $5.95.

Plastic tarps with grommets fitted to them can be bought at little additional cost. But, you will add to their versatility with 'Visklamps.' These little things work. They make attaching guys unrealistically easy and possible at any point on the entire sheet. On top of these advantages, once you've got your shelter set up, and the wind changes the direction of the rain, you can quickly move the whole thing around by moving a klamp or two.

To use Visklamps you simply wrap the rubber ball in the sheeting you want to secure and twist it a few times in order to isolate the ball in a kind of node. Pass the ball through the larger section of the Visklamp

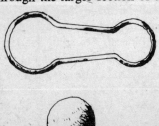

and then down the connecting passage to the smaller section like a garter. Attaching guys or bungee cords to the large empty loop allows you to support the fly in any number of shapes. With three piece sectioned poles you can omit the middle section of a pole set, alter the Visklamp arrangement and lower the profile of the shelter for rain blown by a heavy wind. Any number of misshapen roofs are possible, especially if you add extra pole grommets to the corners of the fly.

There are a couple of other kinds of light weight tarps that should be mentioned. The first is the 'Space Rescue Blanket' from NCR. It shouldn't be mistaken for a polyethylene sheet, as it is a piece of equipment designed for emergency use. Space blankets fit in the palm of your hand when folded, are completely waterproof and fragile because of their thickness, .0005 of an inch. The 'Rescue Blanket' measures 56" x 84", weighs two ounces and is $3.00 from L. L. Bean.

A second more durable kind of 'space blanket' is manufactured by the Thermos people. Much thicker and more durable, the blanket is also 56" x 84" but weighs eleven ounces and costs $7.95, again from L. L. Bean. This laminated blanket is really effective in retaining warmth or reflecting the heat of the sun, and its fibrous core makes it very strong.

PONCHOS

Using a poncho for contingency shelter is much like using a rain-fly, but you save in weight in that a poncho will also protect you if you want to keep moving. Even more pronounced than with a fly is the feeling of waiting out, rather than being protected from, the rain. But a really large poncho, measuring about 8' x 4', will do the job. A poncho, of course, must be pitched very low so as to cover enough area underneath it.

Again, even if you're carrying other shelter you should get a poncho with grommets or have them added so it can serve as gear and vehicle protection.

There are three basic kinds of ponchos. Army issue are made of rubberized fabrics, are very strong, heavy, and bulky. These are tough enough to double as ground sheets used to protect your air mattress or delicate and expensive nylon bag. Your local Army-Navy store has them or they can be obtained from the Smilie Company: $7.95.

Nylport or some other variety of coated nylon poncho is probably the best, but they are expensive. Some can be had with sleeves and even large front pockets, but be sure that yours will open completely into a flat sheet. One from Moor and Mountain is Nylport: 7'4" x 3'9" $17.00.

Plastic ponchos, like poly-tarps, are light, cheap and waterproof but extremely fragile. You can get them from Smilie at $3.00.

TUBE TENTS

Tube tents are a little closer in design to a full fledged tent. Most of them are made of the same three or four millimeter plastic material that is found in plastic sheeting, and they are just as waterproof and delicate to the touch. Every catalogue offering them illustrates one strung between two perfectly placed trees as though the world were built for hammocks. Bring poles.

Tube tent dimensions are given as length and circumference, a third of the latter being the usual width of the floor. Highland Outfitters offers the one-man variety 9½' long x 9' circumference, 1 lb. 4 oz., $1.60. Vinyl and slightly stronger one and two-man models can be had from Holubar:

9½' x 9'	1 lb. 7 oz.	$2.00
9½' x 12'	2 1	3.00

Trailwise, sold by the Ski Hut, makes a durable, more sophisticated version. This tube tent is urethane coated fabric throughout, with heavier material used for the floor, and it even has peg loops and pull-outs on the sides. The floor is eighty-six inches in length and fifty-eight inches wide at the front, tapering to forty-two inches at the rear. The height is forty-two inches at the front and drops to thirty-six inches at the rear. This almost-tent weighs two pounds, two ounces and costs $17.00. If you were to sew netting into the front and rear you'd have an even more effective shelter.

Another high quality almost-tent is the 'Gerry Pioneer.' Pitched as a two-man, it has no floor but when only one man need use it, the coated side walls fold under and zip together, effectively sealing the inside off from ground water Two of them can be zipped together to make a large three-man shelter. It comes with netted end walls and laid out flat measures 106 inches by 102 inches. The 'Pioneer' weighs only one pound, eleven ounces and Gerry suggests its retail price as $35.00

POLES AND PEGS

I've already mentioned the reasoning behind carry-

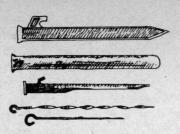

ing poles and pegs as not only convenient but often as ecologically more sound. With that, you only need know where to get them.

There seem to be innumerable varieties of weights and corresponding strengths in tent poles, but there are really only two basic kinds. The first sort is sectioned aluminum. They come in two or three detachable pieces and sometimes have shock cord through the hollow center of the pieces to insure that no one section gets lost. This makes them easier to assemble too.

For quite a while I preferred the more easily jammed telescoping variety because if I were going to lose something vital like a tent pole, I wanted to lose all of it. Reinforcing this logic was the argument that it is worse to lose just one section of a pole and thus render it useless than to have the whole thing jam and so become dead weight. Now that poles come tied together, I think this system best. It's too bad I can't afford them.

Everybody sells poles. Highland Outfitters is one of the many distributors with a wide selection. Prices run as follows:

Aluminum Tent Poles

3'6"	3 sections	7 ounces	$2.19
4'	3	8	2.35
4'6"	4	9	2.75
5'	4	11	2.98
6'	4	15	3.95

The Ski Hut sells poles with top fittings that allow you to turn them into 'A' frame supports. This angle design is a little more expensive, but if you use one set at the entrance, the shelter will be a lot easier to get into and out of. A straight '1' will do at the rear. If you've got a really large nylon fly or tarp, a second set of angled poles can be erected at the midpoint along the ridge line to hold it up or even make it larger than the entrance, giving the floor plan something of the shape of Alpine Design's 'Yosemite' tent.

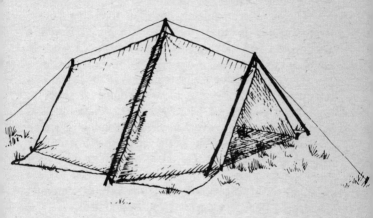

Pegs come in all sorts of designs: round, nail, skewer, stake, and special snow pegs. They can also be bought in aluminum, plastic, and steel. The plastic ones usually come in orange or yellow, making them a little more difficult to lose and unlike thin, ultralight aluminum skewers, plastic pegs can be driven in with a big rock. They, too, can be had from any retailer and cost anywhere from 7¢ to 45¢ apiece. The plastic ones cost about 20¢.

Guy line tighteners are handy little devices that

weigh nothing and help those who have trouble with knots. They make it easy to measure the form and tension of your shelter. They effect a sort of slip knot in the line which can be fixed at any point once the tent is guyed. Some are triangular, some straight, and others bent. They all work pretty well, arguments about them arising mostly from mountaineers who find themselves in gale force winds which can pull some lose. Generally, they cost about a nickel apiece. Eastern Mountain Sports sells them in both nylon and aluminum with two or three holes, as you please.

If you're economizing on your roof, try not to skimp on the paraphernalia for pitching it. Even a plastic sheet will hide you from the rain if it's securely guyed.

These needn't be ineffective roofs. Plan ahead and set up whatever rig you choose a couple of times to make sure you've got what you need. These shelters have weight in their favor. If you're pedaling or riding a motorcycle that is a bit on the small size, a pound or two can make a difference. More important than their weight is their price. It might be a good idea to stop sometime during the summer, take the $10.00 you didn't spend on a backpacking tent, and buy a steak.　　●

Tents

TENT	LENGTH	FRONT WIDTH OR WIDEST POINT	REAR WIDTH	PEGS	FRONT HEIGHT OR HIGHEST POINT	REAR HEIGHT
BISHOP'S						
Pack-Lite	7'	5'	5'	10	52"	52"
Camp-Lite	7'	5'	5'	10	52"	52"
BLACK'S						
Tunnel	7'	4' 3"	4' 3"	None	39"	39"
Wren	8'	4'	4'	16	40"	40"
Itisa	6' 6"	6'	6'	15	66"	—
Standard	5'	7'	7'	16	60"	—
SIERRA DESIGNS						
3-Man Hexagonal	7'	8'	4'	9	67"	—
EUREKA						
Two-Man Mountain	6' 4"	5'	5'	8	42"	42"
Mt. Marcy	8'	5'	5'	14	42"	42"
Mt. Katahdin	8'	5'	5'	20	42"	42"
Two-Man Alpine	7' 9"	5'	5'	None	48"	30"
One-Man High-Lite	7' 2"	3' 6"	2' 6"	16	36"	21"
GERRY						
Lodgepole	7' 2"	4'	4'	8	38"	26"
Fireside	8'	6'	6'	8	49"	34"
Yearound	6'10"	4'	4'	8	43"	24"
Camponaire	8'	5'	5'	10	72"	24"
Fortnight	9'	8'	8'	10	72"	36"
ALPINE DESIGNS						
Yosemite 2-Man	6' 6"	4' 8"	2' 9"	None	54"	28"
Yosemite 3-Man	7'	6' 2	3'10"	None	60"	31"
Timberline	7'	4' 6"	4' 6"	None	4"	33"
Alpine	7' 9"	4' 5"	4' 5"	12	46"	32"

COMMENTS	WEIGHT	WATERPROOF SIDEWALLS
Screened doors front and rear,	6 lbs. 8 oz.	12″
External poles and side pulls	9 lbs. 12½ oz.	12″
	12 lbs. 8 oz.	No
	15 lbs. 12 oz.	No
External poles available for both these	9 lbs. 4 oz.	Silicone Treated
center peak tents	8 lbs. 12 oz.	No
38″ Cookhole included, three external poles	6 lbs. 8 oz.	14″
	7 lbs.	None
Single wall, coated nylon	4 lbs. 8 oz.	Throughout
Breatheable Mt. Marcy with fly sheet	4 lbs. 12 oz.	12″
Blanchard, external frame design	8 lbs. 8 oz.	18″
Front angle pole included	3 lbs. 4 oz.	None
Permanently attached fly sheet	3 lbs. 8 oz.	None
Permanently attached fly sheet	4 lbs. 8 oz.	None
Triangular front vestibule	5 lbs. 2 oz.	6″
External pole peak tent	7 lbs. 12 oz.	6″
External pole peak tent	10 lbs. 5 oz.	6″
	5 lbs. 14 oz.	4″
30″ additional length in vestibule	7 lbs.	4″
35″ additional length in vestibule	3 lbs. 14 oz.	13″
36″ additional length in vestibule	4 lbs. 7 oz.	12″

PACKED SIZE	TENT FLOOR MATERIAL	TENT WALL MATERIAL	REAR VENT (Screened)
23"x4"	1.7 oz. White Ripstop	0.9 oz. Ripstop	Door
23"x7"	6 oz. Blue Nylon	5.4 oz. Poplin	Door
24"x8"	5.5 oz. Yellow Cotton	5.5 oz. Yellow Cotton	8"x12" optional
20"x7"	1.5 oz. Yellow Ripstop	1.5 oz. Yellow Ripstop	8"x12" optional
24"x8"	3.25 oz. Blue Cotton	3.25 oz. Blue Cotton	8"x12" optional
23"x6"	3.25 oz. Tan Cotton	3.25 oz. Tan Cotton	8"x12" optional
24"x8"	Nylport	1.9 oz. Ripstop	Triangle
21"x4"	6.5 oz. Poplin	6.5 oz. Poplin	None
23"x4"	1.7 oz. Ripstop	1.4 oz. Ripstop	Triangle
17"x8"	1.7 oz. Ripstop	1.5 oz. Ripstop	Triangle
24"x6"	1.7 oz. Ripstop	6.5 oz. Poplin	Window
20"x3"	1.7 oz. Ripstop	2.2 oz. Ripstop	Window
16"x5"	2 oz. Nylon	2 oz. Taffeta Nylon	Window
17"x7"	2 oz. Nylon	2 oz. Taffeta Nylon	Window
16"x6"	2 oz. Nylon	2 oz. Taffeta Nylon	Window
16"x8"	2 oz. Nylon	2 oz. Taffeta Nylon	Window
16"x11"	2 oz. Nylon	2 oz. Taffeta Nylon	Window
18"x5"	Ripstop Nylon	1.5 oz. Dacron-Cotton	Window
18"x7"	Ripstop Nylon	1.5 oz. Dacron-Cotton	Window
18"x6"	K-Kote Nylon	2 oz. Nylon Taffeta	Window
18"x6"	K-Kote Nylon	2 oz. Nylon Taffeta	Window

PRICE	FLY WEIGHT	FLY PRICE	TOTAL WEIGHT	TOTAL PRICE
$104.50	2 lb.	Included	8 lbs. ½ oz.	$104.50
53.50	2 lb.	45.00	11 lbs. 12½ oz.	98.50
$119.50	None	None	12 lbs. 8 oz.	$119.50
75.95	Included	Included	15 lbs. 12 oz.	75.95
95.00	4 lb.	59.95	13 lbs. 4 oz.	154.95
85.00	4 lb.	43.50	12 lbs. 12 oz.	136.50
$155.00	1½ lb.	Included	8 lbs. 4 oz.	$155.00
$ 21.95	None	None	7 lbs.	$ 21.95
39.95	None	None	4 lbs. 8 oz.	39.95
59.95	Included	Included	4 lbs. 12 oz.	59.95
69.00		13.50	13 lbs. 4 oz.	82.50
49.95	12 oz.	19.95	4 lbs.	69.90
$ 70.00	Included	Included	3 lbs. 8 oz.	$ 70.00
90.00	Included	Included	4 lbs. 8 oz.	90.00
100.00	Included	Included	5 lbs. 2 oz.	100.00
140.00	Included	Included	7 lbs. 12 oz.	140.00
195.00	Included	Included	10 lbs. 5 oz.	195.00
	Included	Included	5 lbs. 14 oz.	$110.00
	Included	Included	7 lbs.	135.00
$100.00	1 lb. 4 oz.	Included	5 lbs. 2 oz.	100.00
117.50	1 lb.	Included	5 lbs. 7 oz.	117.50

Tents

TENT	LENGTH	FRONT WIDTH OR WIDEST POINT	REAR WIDTH	PEGS	FRONT HEIGHT OR HIGHEST POINT	REAR HEIGHT
CAMP TRAILS						
Chaparral	7'	4' 6"	4' 6"	10	44"	40"
Two-Man Backpacker	7'	4' 6"	4' 6"	10	40"	36"
THERMOS						
Pop Tent: Hex-Dome	6' 9"	7' 10"	3' 10"	None	56"	—
Pocket Camper	—	7' 9"	3' 8"	None	42"	—
ALASKA						
Family 3-Man	8'	6'	6'	8	60"	32"
High Lakes 2-Man	8'	5'	5'	11	48"	48"
Packer	7'	4' 2"	2' 6"	8	48"	30"
RECREATIONAL EQUIPMENT						
Two-Man	7' 4"	4' 6"	4' 6"	14	48"	36"
High-Ender	7'	4' 10"	4' 10"	14	44"	44"
High-Light	7'	5' 2"	5' 2"	14	44"	44"
TRAILWISE						
Two-Man	7' 5"	4' 8"	4' 8"	12	48"	48"
HIMALAYAN						
Two-Man				7		
Three-Man				7		
WHITE STAG						
Alpine	7' 4"	5' 10"	5' 10"	12	42"	42"
WARMLITE						
Model 6 Sc	11' 2"	5'	5'	3	40"	28"
Model 7 Sc	12' 6"	5'	5'	3	40"	40"
Model 8 Sc	15' 4"	7' 6"	7' 6"	3	45"	45"
HOLUBAR						
Royalite	7' 6"	5'	4'	None	54"	30"

WATERPROOF SIDEWALLS	WEIGHT	COMMENTS
Foam laminated roof, single wall. Coated nylon, single wall	4 lbs. 3 lbs. 13 oz.	Throughout Throughout
Fiberglass ribs support both of these hexagonal domes	16 lbs. 9 lbs.	Throughout Throughout
	8 lbs. 4 lbs. 4 lbs. 12 oz.	6" 10" 6"
External angle poles Huge screened side windows	3 lbs. 8 oz. 4 lbs. 12 oz. 6 lbs. 6 oz.	8" None None
Both tunnel door and flap door included	5 lbs. 8 oz.	13"
External hoop supports, both these tents shaped very much like warmlites.	2 lbs. 4 oz. 2 lbs. 9 oz.	
	5 lbs.	6"
Very large with hoop supports Very, very large Huge	2 lbs. 7 oz. 3 lbs. 6 oz. 4 lbs. 14 oz.	Throughout Throughout Throughout
Angled poles	3 lbs. 15 oz.	12"

PACKED SIZE	TENT FLOOR MATERIAL	TENT WALL MATERIAL	REAR VENT (Screened)
15"x7"	1.5 oz. Ripstop	1.5 oz. Ripstop	Window
15"x6"	1.5 oz. Ripstop	1.5 oz. Ripstop	Window
30"x8"	Vinyl Nylon	8.16 oz. Cotton Drill	Window
24"x6"	Vinyl Nylon	8.16 oz. Cotton Drill	None
24"x7"	Nylon	Nylon	Window
22"x4"	Nylon	Nylon	Window
22"x4"	Nylon	Nylon	Window
16"x5"	Nylon	Nylon	Tunnel Vent
17"x7"	Nylon	Nylon	Tunnel Vent
18"x7"	Nylon	Nylon	None
18"x6"	1.9 oz. Ripstop	1.9 oz. Ripstop	Tunnel Door
15"x4"	1.2 oz. Ripstop	1.2 oz. Ripstop	None
16"x4"	1.2 oz. Ripstop	1.2 oz. Ripstop	None
18"x6"	Nylon	Nylon	Window
15"x5"	1.2 oz. Ripstop	1.2 oz. Ripstop	Window
16"x7"	1.2 oz. Ripstop	1.2 oz. Ripstop	Window
18"x9"	1.2 oz. Ripstop	1.2 oz. Ripstop	Window
24"x7"	1.9 oz. Ripstop	1.9 oz. Ripstop	Window

PRICE	FLY WEIGHT	FLY PRICE	TOTAL WEIGHT	TOTAL PRICE
$ 90.00	None	None	4 lbs.	$ 96.00
80.75	None	None	3 lbs. 13 oz.	80.75
$ 61.95	None	None	16 lbs.	$ 61.95
39.95	None	None	9 lbs.	39.95
$150.00	Included	Included	8 lbs.	$150.00
85.00	Included	Included	4 lbs.	85.00
79.95	Included	Included	4 lbs. 12 oz.	79.95
$ 73.50	1 lb. 6 oz.	Included	4 lbs. 14 oz.	$ 73.50
78.50	1 lb. 12 oz.	Included	6 lbs. 8 oz.	78.50
73.50	None	None	6 lbs. 6 oz.	73.50
$106.00	1 lb. 12 oz.	$30.00	7 lbs. 4 oz.	$135.00
$120.00	14 oz.	Included	3 lbs. 2 oz.	$120.00
160.00	14 oz.	Included	3 lbs. 8 oz.	160.00
$ 60.00	Included	Included	5 lbs.	$ 60.00
$122.00	None	None	2 lbs. 7 oz.	$122.00
156.00	None	None	3 lbs. 6 oz.	156.00
204.00	None	None	4 lbs. 14 oz.	204.00
$105.00	1 lb. 6 oz.	Included	5 lbs. 5 oz.	$105.00

Sleeping Bags

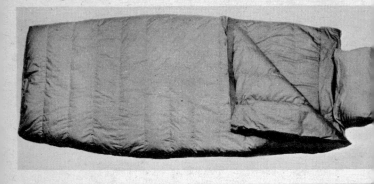

by Peter W. Tobey

Selecting a sleeping bag is a great place to save some money, until it's time to go to sleep. Then anyone who has ventured out with something about as effective as army blankets will know he's blown the most important choice of camping equipment.

Most of the modern developments in bag design have been prompted by backpacking needs. Weight and bulk are at extraordinary premiums in backpacking and manufacturers cut every ounce possible from their products. As a result there is great concentration on insulator efficiency and nearly all high quality bags are filled with that rare and expensive natural insulator, pure goose down.

The camping bicyclist or motorcyclist comes to this market with needs that are similar to the backpacker's but which are less extreme. The two wheel traveler, especially the motorcyclist, who travels in summer can sacrifice some of the luxuries of down and get a good bag much more cheaply by turning to other materials. But he should know what a good bag is regardless of what kind of insulation is used. In deciding on a foam, synthetic fiber or feather bag you should know just how much you're giving up. And to know that, you should be aware of the factors that make a good bag.

A sleeping bag doesn't warm you, it holds your body heat. In other words, a bag doesn't generate any heat, it conserves what you've got. What's more, it's the dead or still air held by the insulation of a bag which keeps you warm, not the insulating material itself. Any insulation which will hold a blanket of non-circulating air around your body will be effective. The thicker the blanket of air, the more heat will be retained by the bag. It's as simple as that.

Rolled newspapers, dry grass or leaves, anything that will compartmentalize and therefore immobilize air between the inner and outer layers of the bag will work. The U. S. Army Quartermaster, in recording the insulation necessary for comfort at various temperatures, lists them by thickness:

Temperature	40° F.	20°	0°	—20°
Insulation Loft	1.5″	2.0″	2.5″	3.0″

The question is not one of effectiveness, (six inches of any insulation is about as effective as six inches of down) but it's a question of efficiency, and the criterion of bag insulation that make it efficient are best met by pure down.

Certainly the bicyclist and to a large extent the motorcyclist as well, find weight important. Lofted or fully expanded down is extremely light by volume. Thus, the amount of air held by a pound of down is greater than that held by other insulators and so it traps more heat. Swiss Ski Imports lists the following insulation to weight values, based simply enough on how much volume there is to one pound of insulation:

Down	100%	Acetate Fibre	44%
Polyester Fibre	71%	Wool	32%

Down is the most compressible of insulators. It is also extremely resilient, that is, it rebounds from being repeatedly compressed and lofted during use. The gradual loss of this ability to spring back after being compressed and released results in other materials in the loss of their original thickness. This in spite of the fact they did not compress so well as down when new. The effect is that down stays a better insulator longer, and when it is not in use it can be packed up smaller.

Warmth is only one of the factors in sleeping comfort. You also have to stay dry. Down allows the moisture that the body gives off to pass quickly to the outside of the bag. It does so by maintaining a certain level of moisture at all times and naturally correcting changes in that level. If it is soaked or artificially dried beyond its normal moisture range it will quickly return to its natural moisture content. This property of down keeps moisture build up in the bag from causing clammy, chilling nights. It also keeps the down from becoming wet and heavy and so losing its loft.

Bags with waterproof shells will not allow body moisture to escape, regardless of what insulation is used. Similarly, bags with rubber or plastic bottoms have something of the same effect and when they do get wet, do not dry nearly so quickly. Water is heavy, and over a period of a few days a sleeping bag can absorb and hold two or three pounds of water.

No matter what insulation a bag has, you should inquire into its washability. The oils in down are a little sensitive, but with care it can be washed and machine dried. Most synthetics require almost as much gentle treatment. Though in the past most manufacturers have discouraged the dry cleaning of down filled bags and jackets, many cleaners have now become experienced in this art. The danger comes with nonpetroleum based cleaning agents. Since most commercial cleaners use such cleaning agents, they must show special care.

Down bags can be washed at home very easily. Soaps, not detergents, should be used in cool water and drying should be accomplished at low heats and over a long time if necessary. Adding a few tennis balls to the drier will break up wet lumps of down in tumbling and also set up static electrical charges that contribute to full lofting.

Air circulation is an important factor in the long life of down products, because no substance, no matter how tough, is perfectly resilient. For these reasons down and most other insulations as well should be stored loosely in an area where air can circulate freely. The rolling of the bag when in use is one thing, but storing it in a small, waterproof stuff sack for months on end may be damaging. Mildew that develops when the bag is damp may permanently reduce its loft.

With enough study and comparison you can finally nit pick your way into real silliness. In an article like this that kind of overkill is an annoying possibility, but if you're buying a really excellent bag you may spend a hundred dollars or more, and a hundred dollars or more should buy a lot of nifty detail.

One distinction that seems trivial but isn't, is that between goose and duck down. Duck down is lighter than synthetics for comparable comfort ranges but is about 80% as efficient as pure, well processed goose down. Duck down bags can be a reasonable compromise when the problem of money arises, but don't assume you'll save. Some outlets sell duck for as much as goose down and you certainly get something less.

There is even more of a difference between down and feathers. Even curled or crushed feathers are not as efficient an insulator as down.

And finally, a really slight difference in grades of down for the sake of thoroughness: Mixtures of down and feathers vary. So also do the size of the feathers, which by legal definition include very soft, ¼ inch specimens that are to be too small to be removed from even the best down. Most suppliers produce down in two grades: One with from 12-20% feathers for down bags, and one with 8-11% for garments. Of the many brands we've studied, Holubar's are the only ones using the higher grade garment down. They contend that the slight loss in loft speed is negligible, and the gains in efficiency are worth the expense. With most down products efficiency varies directly with cost, and Holubar's excellent products are very efficient.

There are many other insulators used in sleeping bags. Products like 'Dacron 88', 'Cumuloft', and 'Equitherm' are among the many which are effective and much less expensive than down. Many brands of both synthetic foam and fiber are used, but they are generally about half as efficient. As a rule they weigh twice as much and do not compress so well, and so are bulkier.

One high quality synthetic insulator that should be mentioned is 'Fiberfill II' by Dupont. It is a light weight polyester that rivals down for resiliency and compression if not for weight. Because of the weight factor you probably shouldn't expect a bag of the weight needed in mountain climbing with this insulation to be able to cope with winter conditions. But for summer use, and especially on a motorcycle, a bag of this design is much cheaper and very effective. 'Fortrel', from the Celanese Corporation, is also a very good insulator of the same kind.

The type of insulator is not the only factor in the efficiency of a bag. There are compartments which hold the fill in place, keeping it from bunching and leaving thin spots where insulation will be poor. The effectiveness of these compartments will determine how much of any given insulator is needed to maintain an average thickness in the bag.

Of course, the baffles must not allow even small amounts of the insulator to pass through what should be restraining barriers, but water vapor should be able to circulate in order to aid in the breathing of the bag. Both nylon and netting are commonly used. Nylon is generally stronger and does not allow down to sift here and there.

A fantastic number of baffle configurations have been developed. Their varying effectiveness is relative to how evenly they spread the insulation. Very small channels control down thickness better, but the added baffle material weighs more and packs bigger. Well designed channels maintain consistent down thickness without having to use too much baffling material.

Channel tubes with the inner and outer walls sewn directly together leave thin, cold spots. However, for summer use, this design is cheap and adequate, especially if the bag has a separate outer shell.

There are three very light, very effective systems: the box, the parallelogram, and the overlapping triangular channels.

231

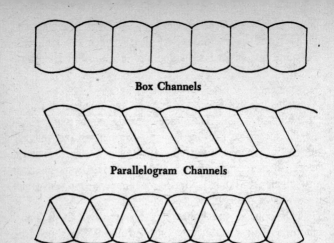

Box Channels

Parallelogram Channels

Triangular Channels

The other distinct type is the laminated or double quilt design. It is two simply sewn channel systems one inside the other and is both heavy and bulky.

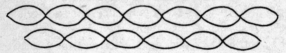

Channels can be laid out on the bag in a number of ways, but there are three basic types. Longitudinal baffling allows a gradual migration of down to the foot of the bag every time you get in it.

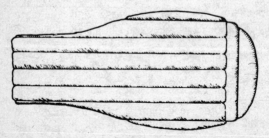

Transverse channeling puts a stop to that.

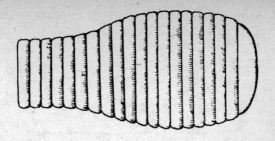

And the Chevron design is even more effective.

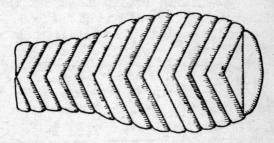

Shell and liner fabric also play their role in different bag designs. Primarily, they must be both strong and light. But they must also serve to curb heat loss through radiation, absorb moisture, and feel nice.

Just what feels best is a matter of preference, but cotton liners are more like bed sheets and people generally prefer them. However, nylon is a lot tougher, especially ripstop nylon; it's also lighter and very breatheable. Coated nylon bags are a bad idea. Their water repellancy causes condensation inside the bag and you can end up swimming in your own sweat.

Another aspect of design is the relationship between the size of the inside of the bag and the size of the outside. Many fine bags are cut 'differentially', with the outside shell larger than the inside liner. Differential cutting aids in lofting, and helps keep knees and elbows from compressing the lofted insulation by restraining them with a smaller interior.

The alternative 'flat' cut allows freer body movement, while the internal volume of the bag is reduced as added material fills empty spaces with folds in the liner and expanded down. In these bags baffling systems must prevent thin spots.

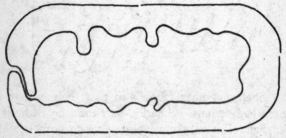

If you like the differential cutting theory but also like stretching and rolling around in your sleep, consider buying from a manufacturer who will custom size a bag or one who stocks over-sized equipment.

It should be pretty clear by now that just how warm you'll stay in a sleeping bag depends on a lot of things. The overall shape of the bag is right up there with other essential considerations.

The best known sleeping bag shape is the Boy Scout rectangle. It roughly contains the human form and is simple and inexpensive to make. From the standpoint of thermal efficiency it is a throwback to mule and blanket days, but in spite of all the modern mountaineer's logic it has its adherents and for good reason.

In the same way the smaller interiors of differentially cut bags are somewhat confining, so too is the contoured shape of the 'mummy bag.' Foetal positions, stretching, and even the most elementary of friendly activities are nearly impossible in a mummy. Another distinction between the two types is that with a rectangular bag, when you roll over, the bag doesn't. A mummy fits closely, so, when you move, so will it. It's not a big thing and the mummy doesn't take long to get used to, but of such trivia choices are made.

The sales personnel who wait on the unsuspecting cyclist in most of this country's light weight camping gear retail stores are backpackers and mountaineers. They invariably suggest the mummy-shaped bag, mostly because they're specialists in coping with extreme circumstances, especially those where even slight comfort is hard won rather than easily found. They choose the mummy because it is lighter, less bulky and considerably warmer for any given loft, since there is less interior space and less outside surface area from which heat may escape.

There is no question that mummies are best for retaining body warmth. But there is a compromise and it inevitably comes in the form of bags dubbed 'semirectangular'. These are narrow rectangular bags, with tapered feet, which have a little more roominess but warm a little less efficiently than the mummy style. Both the semirectangular and mummy bags can be, but are not always, equipped with combinations of zippers so as to allow plenty of ventilation in warm weather. If your bag is for summer use and you'd like the advantages of down, then consider that any bag gets hot on a warm evening. The extreme of versatility in these circumstances is one with a full length zipper that goes completely around the foot of the bag so that it can be opened into a quilt or comforter and used as such in the summer.

Finally, and to the point, every type of bag can be ordered in complementary pairs which zip together, and one piece double mummies are available.

Because sleeping bags do not generate, but hold warmth produced by the body, factors like metabolism rates and body surface to weight ratios of the sleeper have a considerable effect on the temperature inside. Wind and humidity are also important factors. As a result, simple formulas relating fill weights to the lowest temperatures at which the bag is still comfortable are crude at best. Most retailers quote the saw: Two pounds of down for summer use and three pounds for temperatures as low as 0°.

The chart below is a compilation from the conservative claims of reputable manufacturers. Keep in mind that the problem of being too warm can be virtually eliminated by ordering a bag with a full length zipper, a sensible five-dollar addition that weighs only five ounces extra.

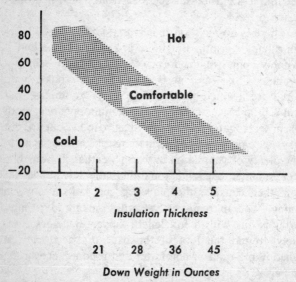

Mountaineering bags are specialized equipment which are not only superexpensive but are also useless in the summer. A bag designed for cold weather with as much as four or five pounds of down fill, will roast you in warm weather even when equipped with two-way full length zippers. Low fill weight bags, with one and a half or two pounds of down will serve very well for most summer conditions. A slightly heavier bag will be more versatile to a point, but the efficiencies of modern bags make them very warm, so consider when you'll use them and where.

Summer conditions and a shortage of money make synthetic fills a likely alternative. The Boy Scouts of America make some pretty good bags filled with virgin polyesters, 'Dacron 88,' and 'Astrofill' which sell for fifteen to twenty-five dollars and weigh from five to six pounds. For the catalogue write to:

> Boy Scouts of America
> 316 Main Street
> Ridgefield, Connecticut   06877

Coleman is another maker of reasonable durable synthetically filled bags. Their line starts with a small 'Acryfill' bag for $9.95 and offers a good selection through the mail from:

> H & H Surplus & Camper's Haven
> 305 West Baltimore Street
> Baltimore, Maryland   21201

Good bags last, and if you're beginning to feel like a confirmed nomad; a nylon shelled, down filled bag may be worth it. But if you've a big motorcycle or strong legs and no money, the synthetics will work well under the conditions for which they are designed. Regardless, when you go to buy a bag, consider its functions and efficiencies in terms of your own trade-offs in price and durability.

BAGS

Gerry

Gerry is one of the oldest of the sleeping bag manufacturers. Not only did they begin the trend towards semirectangular bags, but they now fill them with a wide variety of insulations. Their semirectangular series, known as 'Zipair' bags, includes the 'Wilderness,' which is filled with goose down, the 'Yosemite' and 'Appalachian,' which contain duck down, and the 'Quetico' which is made of 'Dacron 88.'

The series' greatest strength is that each of its bags is the same size and has the same zippers. Thus, any bag can be fully opened and zipped to any other in order to form a double bag. The advantage of their being interchangeable is that a very lightweight bag, like the Appalachian can be the top bag in the summer and a heavier bag, like the Wilderness, will be warm enough to serve on top in the winter. You need only turn the pair over.

This system works well because even the heaviest winter bag is compressed on the bottom layer once you get into it. Your weight presses down its loft so it no longer insulates and you require a mattress or pad of some kind. This factor makes it relatively unimportant how thick the bottom layer is when fully lofted and so a thinner bag, like the Appalachian is satisfactory.

The Quetico is decidedly a summer bag. Its insulation is composed of a good synthetic and it is extremely well made of two ounce nylon taffeta and all nylon zippers. For $35.00 you can hardly beat it.

Gerry's higher priced mummies, like the 'Olympic' and 'X-19,' are mountain-oriented. Unless you expect your bag to serve on both mountains and bikes, the Zipair series is probably a better choice.

Gerry's catalogue is uninspired and so not so helpful as it might be. But it has good things in it. Their tents, I can't help thinking, are better than their bags, but the tents are relatively more expensive and so ought to be. Send for the catalogue and look at both.

> Gerry
> 5450 North Valley Highway
> Denver, Colorado   80216

North Face

These are sleeping bags of excellent design and construction. One of their best features is the coil zippers used throughout. Nylon coil zippers are the best method of opening and closing sleeping bags. Rather than having individual teeth which are pressed into the tape, continuous coils are woven into the tape itself. This eliminates the problem of teeth breaking or falling out and allows the zipper to turn corners with less resistance. The best of the coil's qualities is that it is extremely gentle on fabric. Even if you snag a hunk of light weight nylon you can simply pull it out of the zipper without tearing a hole in the liner.

The 'Superlight' is a slim cut mummy that has a minimum of weight and bulk. Designed for moderate temperatures, it has less than two pounds of fill and yet warms to about 20°. If mummies don't bother you and you're traveling on two wheels, this is about as fine a bag as you can get for the money.

Two bags of identical design that are well suited to the tourist are the 'Unimog' and the 'Minimog.' The Unimog is a luxurious, down-filled bag that's very warm. The Minimog contains duck down and so is ideal for milder temperatures. Both will open completely and zip together so that there are zipper openings on each side. Thus, either you or your friend can separately control the temperature.

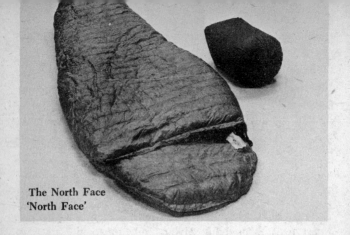

The North Face
'North Face'

The North Face's is a very interesting catalogue, with pictures as good as anyone's and some very close detail.

The North Face
308 Columbus Avenue
San Francisco, California   94133

Sierra Design

Sierra Design's bags are mountain-oriented equipment, very light and slim cut for the least possible bulk. The '100,' '200,' and '300' series are all extremely close cut bags that will annoy anyone who finds the tight quarters of a mummy confining. But for the bicyclist especially, these are attractive extremes.

The seventy-inch side zipper adds to the versatility of the bags and allows them to be zipped together.

Sierra's more general purpose bags share the expedition mummy bags' quality, but are considerably more versatile. Both the 'Omni' and the 'Omni Light' open flat and can be doubled. Their only drawback is that they are short bags and so a little foot tight for a big man.

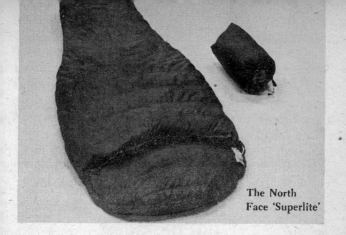

The North
Face 'Superlite'

Holubar and Sierra make the best of the double mummies.

The Sierra Design catalogue is closer to art than information. It is an attractive black and white presentation of the relatively few high quality goods they offer. The cover could double for a high school literary magazine, and it fits right into the decor on any well-appointed coffee table. There are nice looking girls in it too.

Sierra Designs Inc.
Fourth and Addison Streets
Berkeley, California   94710

Alpine Designs

There are some very appealing design characteristics in these bags. The 'Woodsman' has snap-in fittings for cotton-dacron liners that are used by many campers to keep their bags clean. These liners are easily removed and laundered. The Woodsman also comes in a shape very close to rectangular and, therefore, is roomy, yet it has an effective, integral hood for cold weather.

Another welcome variation is the 'Trail Sleeper's' duck down. This is a high quality, rectangular bag that is ideal for summer use. The duck down is very efficient and compressible, but it is considerably less expensive than standard goose-down-filled bags. It will open completely, and can be zippered to a matching bag to form a double.

Alpine Designs offers a super-high-powered-deluxe-advertisement-oriented catalogue. It has fairly good descriptions of a number of acceptable bags.

> Alpine Designs
> Box 1081
> Boulder, Colorado   80302

Holubar

Holubar makes the best sleeping bags in the world, one at a time, by hand. The company is a small one that, like the makers of Bishop's tents, produces what they honestly consider to be the 'ultimate.' Anything built with this sort of uncompromising attention to detail and design is bound to be expensive. You can pay an im-

The Sierra Designs 'Double Mummy'

pressive and uncompromising $165.00 for the Holubar custom made 'Ultimate.' Comfortable to temperatures where tire rubber solidifies, this is twice the bag you need for conditions that any healthy mind would ever subject its body to. But you may enjoy fondling the thing.

You can get Holubar quality for as little as $85.00 in the very light and compact 'Timberline' or at a number of other price-quality levels between it and the Ultimate. One bag especially suited to the summer camper is the 'Ponderosa.' It is fully rectangular and opens completely flat for warm nights. It costs $110.00.

All Holubar bags zip together with any other model. Their catalogue is excellent, particularly its discussion of down sleeping bags.

> Holubar
> Box 7
> Boulder, Colorado 80302

Antarctic Imports

The Antarctica line is made in New Zealand and can be mail ordered from the United States. You can save a good deal by going through the more time consuming process of buying from this outfit for a number of reasons. The simplest of them involve savings of retail markups, import agent fees, wharfage, warehousing, and state sales taxes.

More impressive is the government of New Zealand's efforts to encourage exports. They offer a 20% tax incentive to exporters and Antarctic passes most of this along to the American consumer in hopes of establishing themselves in this country's boom market of camping equipment.

Antarctic's experience with expedition quality gear is long-term, and the materials they use in their bags is among the best. Their design details are comparable to those of the major U.S. firms in quality and the workmanship is excellent.

There is one idiosyncracy in these bag's design: The greater the number of compartments into which the down is divided in a bag the less it will drift and the more constant the loft will be. Making such a bag is more expensive because of the time it takes and the cost of the extra baffling material that must be used. The only difficulty with such a bag is that it is slightly heavier, obviously, because there is more material in it. Antarctic opts for this smaller compartment design.

The Antarctica mummy has a short, thirty inch zipper and so cannot be attached to another matching bag. It comes in blue and costs $46.00 plus a 9½% duty at present.

The tapered rectangular bag is a fine one. Its full length and bottom zipper allows it to be opened into a blanket or zippered to another making a huge double bag. It costs $47.00 plus the 9½% duty.

The Antarctic Imports 'Antarctic Mummy'

You can get information on Antarctic Imports' bags and well laid out instructions on how to mail order them from:

> Antarctic Products, Ltd.
> Box 223
> Nelson, New Zealand

Thomas Black & Sons

Blacks is the oldest of British suppliers. The design of some of their bags is unusual in that they do not taper from head to foot as do the mummy and rectangular shapes. Rather, the hip girth of these bags is the largest, apparently to improve on the confinements of the mummy design without opening the shoulders to cold air. From their shape comes their name: the 'Barrel Cut Icelandic Special.'

The Icelandics are among the few good bags still using 100% Egyptian cotton shells. This is a nice option for those who don't like the feel of nylon. These bags are also among the least expensive of those made of goose down available. For instance, the top of the line, Icelandic Special extra large, costs about $80.00 and the regular model large only $65.00.

> Thomas Black and Sons, Inc.
> 930 Ford Street,
> Ogdensburg, New York   13669

Trailwise

The Ski Hut offers 'Trailwise' equipment. These are very high quality bags, all of which are filled with goose down, have nylon shells and nylon zippers.

The 'Slimline' and 'Norrland' are very similar mountain and backpacking bags. The Norrland is slightly wider for those who feel confined in the close fit of a mummy bag. Each of these models comes in two fill weights, the heavier one for mountain and winter use. They can also be ordered in a variety of lengths.

Trailwise's 'Combi' is a summer bag that is designed for summer use and so may be a good choice for the efficiency-conscious summer cyclist. In addition to having relatively little fill, it opens completely to form a large, soft comforter type blanket when the weather is very warm.

Other than Eastern Mountain Sports' new catalogue, the Ski Hut's is the most colorful and interesting to wish your way through.

> The Ski Hut
> 1615 University Avenue
> Berkeley, California 94703

Sears

It's hard to find a good bag at a low price. Those from the Boy Scouts of America are adequate, dollar for dollar, but won't hold up under hard use. J. C. Penney sells an excellent economy bag, filled with the highly efficient synthetic 'Dacron 88' and designed with a nylon liner and shell. The trouble is J. C. Penney isn't an extensive chain and so the bags are hard to come by. If you get the chance, buy one. These are excellent buys.

The 'Ted Williams' bags from Sears are about the best around for the money that you can mail order easily. Sears manufactures a number of cheap bags, some selling for as little as $6.99, but they're not worth much after only the slightest misuse. The 'Sears' Best' bags are excellent buys, however. They're filled with polyester foam that packs down well and is relatively light. The shells on these bags are 50% polyester and 50% cotton oxford cloth. The liners are made of a very comfortable cotton flannel. The zippers are strong and backed for draft protection. These are summer bags and so it's unlikely you'll have to unzip them for use as a blanket, but they will open completely and two of them can be zipped together.

The bags come in eighty-four- and eighty-nine-inch lengths and in two temperature ranges. The warmer bag is rated effective to thirty degrees and has two top layers and three bottom layers of foam. The bags weigh ten pounds, twelve ounces and eleven pounds and cost $33.75 and $39.75 respectively. The summer weights, effective to temperatures only as low as fifty degrees, have only one top layer and cost $28.75. ●

The Trailwise 'Combi'

Matresses and Pads

One of the major conveniences of down is its compressibility, and all lightweight fills can be stuffed more or less compactly when not in use. Though they are fine insulators when lofted they make lousy padding. They will not support the weight of your shoulders and hips. As a result, some sort of added insulation is essential under any bag suited to two wheel travel. These bags rely on their loft for warmth and the dead air held by the bottom layer of such a bag is easily expelled once you get into it. Not only do they fail to retain body heat, but they cannot support your weight above rough ground.

For any comfort at all you've got to have a mattress or pad. The fabled bed of pine bows, balsam, or moss is damned uncomfortable. It bunches, wanders, and mats down in an hour or two, it will ooze pine sap onto your bag, and it is always perfectly useless insulation because air circulates through it. Balsam and pine boughs are scarce when you need them, especially in America's cloistered, private camp grounds, and they're a nuisance to find and prepare as a mattress.

Most of your weight when sleeping is concentrated on your shoulders and hips. Full length mattresses take up a considerable amount of weight and bulk keeping your feet and knees off the ground when some rolled-up clothes will serve nearly as well. In an effort to avoid this added luggage, backpacker supply houses carry both air mattresses and foam pads in hip lengths. Getting accustomed to sleeping on a short pad is easy and the bicyclist especially should consider this a worthwhile savings in weight.

The most luxurious solution to the problem of comfort is an air mattress. A good one, properly inflated, is better every time than home grown sleeping equipment. The only trick to comfort is to blow it up all the way, get on it and then let air out until your hips and shoulders almost touch the ground. Make it as soft as possible and you'll spread the support of your body over the widest area.

Air mattresses are the most compact of the methods used to keep you off the ground. But, they're the heaviest, and because the air in them is free to circulate, carrying warmth away from your body, they're not such good insulation.

Worse still is their vulnerability. One sharp twig and you're sleeping on the ground by morning. The extreme of this flaw is the plastic air mattress. Though they are cheap and light, unless you can, without second thoughts, plan on a hands-and-knees search and discard routine every night then don't buy one. With any air mattress a ground sheet is almost mandatory protection and a patch kit necessary insurance. With all these extras the direct result of their fragility, you've started to get into a bulk range closer to foam pads.

The toughest air mattress around is Thomas Black's 'Good Companion'. It's made of rubberized cotton canvas, is hip length, and has a pillow compartment that inflates separately and so can be made harder if you like. From Thomas Black or the Ski Hut:

22" x 45"   30 ounces $10.00

Stebco also makes air mattresses. Their full length

models are pretty strong and heavy and come with or without pillows. They start at $5.95 from Eureka.

Much better is Stebco's really durable, lightweight, vinyl-laminated, nylon mattress. From the Ski Hut or Eastern Mountain Sports.

28″ x 50″	28 ounces	$11.00
28″ x 72″	40 ounces	15.00

Open cell foam pads are certainly preferable to air mattresses unless you're an insomniac or like patching holes. They're indestructible, lighter than air mattresses, and only slightly more bulky. Because the pattern of the cells is open, the air can be squeezed out of them if they are rolled very tightly. Thus, they will pack to a four-inch diameter cylinder easily.

The only drawback of open-cell foam is that it will absorb water. These pads should be protected in some way, either by use with a coated ground sheet or by being covered with some waterproof material. Alaska Sleeping Bag covers theirs with coated nylon, while Eastern Mountain Sports sheathes them in a two part nylon bottom and dacron-cotton cover. The untreated top helps to dissipate insensible perspiration. Both come with attached nylon tie straps.

Eastern Mountain Sports' prices are as follows:

1½	20 x 36	$7.00
1½	20 x 42	8
1½	20 x 48	9

2	22 x 54	10.75
2	22 x 60	12.
2	22 x 72	14.00

You can get unsheathed foam pads, some of them are convoluted on their bottom sides.

The only other sort of foam pad has cells which are not connected. These foams, because the air is permanently trapped inside them, are nearly incompressible, like cement. Thus, they are bulky and not at all for softening a bed. Closed-cell foams, however, will not absorb water and are very light. They only exist because mountaineers sleep on glaciers and open-cell foams and air mattresses allow air to circulate under their bags carrying warmth away from their bodies. Closed-cell foams trap this air.

If you are a summer camper these pads are a waste. If you also camp in winter you can buy 'Ensolite' from any mountaineering supplier and varieties of closed-cell foam like 'Thermobar' or the unusually lightweight 'Volarafoam' from Eastern Mountain Sports.

There is one other, quite different way of keeping your bag off the ground. You can get huge hammocks from many suppliers, but mountaineering stores carry some that roll into a ball about the size of your fist. EMS sells a mountain bivouack hammock that I wouldn't want to spend eight hours in for $11.00. The Ski Hut has something in their catalogue they say measures seven feet by twenty feet, weighs only eight ounces and costs $7.00. If you've $7.00 to blow, buy one and let me know what it is like.

Even if you aren't going to try to sleep in it, a hammock can be put to good use keeping food away from animals.

CAMPING AND SURVIVAL BOOKS

Mr. Fletcher walks a lot. Chronicled in *The Man Who Walked Through Time* are his experiences in walking the length of the Grand Canyon National Park, and in *The Thousand Mile Summer* he tells about his trip through the Sierra Range. In *The Complete Walker* he discusses the sport of walking in general.

The important thing to me about Colin Fletcher is that what he likes to do is walk, not survive the sufferings and challenges of the wilderness. He isn't interested in survival techniques nor in improvising boughs and edible plants to his purposes. In this book he tells you very methodically and thoroughly how you can accumulate and use all the stuff needed to live alone and self-contained for weeks on end. Packed, this home of his weighs forty pounds or so. Everything in it is carefully chosen from the best suppliers selling the most modern equipment.

The long, descriptive narratives that follow discussions of what to bring along will actually tell you how to do what you'll need to do if you go walking. A lot of what's covered isn't exactly geared to the cyclist, but the sort of sensible living that is related and the instruction concerning how to manage it yourself apply as soon as you get off the bike.

And you read more than how to do it. Mr. Fletcher is a good writer who walks, not a woodsman who is literate. There's a little lyricism and philosophy mixed with anecdotes that more or less pertain to what he's talking about, and there's a great deal of good humor all through the book. Learning about camping is valuable, but more appealing is getting to know Colin Fletcher. His quirks and concentration on certain odd details are funny and telling. It's a great pleasure to read the writing of a man who thinks very clearly about what he's doing, who thinks about it down to the smallest, most idiosyncratic detail and who then has the good sense to take a little lightly ever having gotten so involved.

Colin Fletcher is a very healthy man. Read his stuff and you'll see.

All of the following books are in print and can be ordered through your local book store. If you've any difficulty getting hold of these or any other camping references, you can order most of them through a number of mountaineering suppliers. Both Eastern Mountain Sports and the Ski Hut have wide selections of good camping and climbing books as well as many on related subjects. Those that you are unlikely to be able to get through book stores can be purchased through mailing addresses and postpaid prices are included with them.

America's Camping Book	Cardwell	Scribners	10.00
Backpack Techniques	Mendenhall	La Siesta	1.00
Backpacking	Rethmel	Burgess	3.75
Camper's Bible	Riviere	Doubleday	1.95
Camping and Woodcraft	Kephart	Macmillan	6.95
The Complete Walker	Colin Fletcher	Knopf	7.95
Coping with Crib-Size Campers	Trost	Stackpole	2.95

Hitchhiker's Hand-book	Grimm	Vagabond Press Box 83 Laguna Beach, California 92652	1.95
How to Stay Alive in the Woods	Angier	Macmillan	.95
Knapsacking Abroad	Klinger	Stackpole	2.95
Lightweight Camping Equipment and How to Make It	Cunningham Hansson	Colorado Outdoor Sports	2.50
The New Way of Wilderness	Rutstrum	Macmillan	4.95
The Potomac Appalachian Trail Club Lightweight Equipment Guide		PATC 1718 North Street, North West Washington, D.C. 20036	1.50
Survival, Evasion and Escape		Superintendent of Documents U.S. Printing Office Washington, D.C. 20402	3.50
Professional Guide's Manual	Herter	Herter's, Inc. Waseca, Minnesota 56093	.45
Sierra Club Wilderness Handbook	Brower	Ballantine	.95
You Can Survive in the Outdoors	Winters	Nugget	2.00

Sleeping Bags

	MINIMUM TEMP	TOP LOFT	FILLING
ALPINE DESIGNS			
Andean	−25°	4½ ″	3 lbs. Goose Down
Nordic	−10°	3½ ″	2 lbs. Goose Down
Sierra	15°	2½ ″	1½ lbs. Goose Down
Woodsman	20°	2½ ″	1¾ lbs. Goose Down
Tundra	20°	2″	2 lbs. Goose Down
Meadow	20°	2″	2 lbs. Goose Down
Trail	20°	2″	2 lbs. Duck Down
GERRY			
Olympic	20°	1¾ ″	1⅝ lbs. Duck Down
Aspen	10°	2″	1¾ lbs. Duck Down
Vail	10°	4″	1¾ lbs. Duck Down
X-19	−15°	5″	2½ lbs. Goose Down
Wilderness	10°	4″	2 lbs. Goose Down
Yosemite	20°	3″	1¾ lbs. Duck Down
Quetico	35°	1½ ″	2¼ lbs. Dacron 88
Appalachian	35°	1¾ ″	1⅜ lbs. Duck Down
WARMLITE			
Solo Single	−20°	3½ ″	1.26-2.34 lbs. Goose Down
Solo Triple	−30°	4½ ″	3.64 lbs. Goose Down
L. L. BEAN			
Mountain Master	− 5°	3½ ″	3 lbs. Duck Down
Mountain Master	10°	2¾ ″	2 lbs. Duck Down
Mountain Master	− 5°	3″	2½ lbs. Duck Down
Mountain Master	10°	2″	1½ lbs. Duck Down
Jen-Cel-Lite	25°	2″	3 lbs. Wool & Polyester
Dacron 88	40°	2″	3 lbs. Dacron 88
HOLUBAR			
Timberline	0°	4″	2¾ lbs. Goose Down
Royalite	−20°	4½ ″	3¼ lbs. Goose Down
Expedition	−30°	5″	4 lbs. Goose Down
Ultimate	−40°	5″	4½ lbs. Goose Down
Ponderosa	10°	2¾ ″	3 lbs. Goose Down
Double Timberline	0°	3″	4½ lbs. Goose Down
CAMP AND TRAIL			
Mountain Top	0°	4″	2 lbs. Goose Down
Nylon Mountain Top	0°	4″	2 lbs. Goose Down
Square Mountain Top	15°	3½ ″	1½ lbs. Goose Down
Couple Bag	0″	3½ ″	2½ lbs. Goose Down

TOTAL WEIGHT	LENGTH	SHOULDER	HIP	FOOT	FOR PEOPLE	BAG SHAPE
4 lbs. 14 oz.	69"	64"	64"	40"	5'10"	Mummy
4 lbs.	69"	64"	64"	40"	5'10"	Mummy
3 lbs. 4 oz.	69"	60"	60"	38"	5'10"	Mummy
3 lbs. 6 oz.	72"	64"	64"	50"	6' 1"	Semi-Rectangular
3 lbs. 4 oz.	73"	65"	65"	36"	6' 1"	Mummy
3 lbs. 6 oz.	73"	64"	64"	52"	6' 1"	Semi-Rectangular
3 lbs. 6 oz.	73"	64"	64"	52"	6' 1"	Semi-Rectangular
3 lbs. 5 oz.	78"	60"	60"	48"	6' 2"	Mummy
3 lbs. 10 oz.	78"	60"	60"	48"	6' 2"	Mummy
3 lbs. 10 oz.	78"	60"	60"	48"	6' 2"	Mummy
4 lbs.	75"	54"	54"	48"	6'	Mummy
4 lbs.	78"	60"	60"	56"	6' 1"	Semi-Rectangular
3 lbs. 15 oz.	78"	60"	60"	56"	6' 1"	Semi-Rectangular
3 lbs. 11 oz.	78"	60"	60"	56"	6' 1"	Semi-Rectangular
3 lbs. 4 oz.	78"	60"	60"	56"	6' 1"	Semi-Rectangular
	89"	64"	64"	44"	6' 1"	Mummy
2 lbs. 7 oz.	89"	64"	64"	44"	6' 1"	Mummy
5 lbs. 12 oz.	84"	66"	66"	66"	6' 2"	Mummy Robe
5 lbs. 3 oz.	84"	66"	66"	66"	6' 2"	Mummy Robe
5 lbs. 3 oz.	76"	66"	66"	66"	6'	Mummy Robe
4 lbs. 8 oz.	76"	66"	66"	66"	6'	Mummy Robe
6 lbs. 12 oz.	77"	60"	60"	60"	6'	Rectangular
6 lbs. 8 oz.	72"	60"	60"	60"	5'11"	Rectangular
4 lbs. 13 oz.	78"	66"	66"	46"	6' 1"	Mummy
5 lbs. 3 oz.	78"	65"	65"	46"	6' 1"	Mummy
6 lbs.	78"	65"	65"	46"	6' 1"	Mummy
6 lbs. 7 oz.	78"	65"	65"	46"	6' 1"	Mummy
5 lbs. 11 oz.	80"	65"	65"	65"	6' 2"	Rectangular
8 lbs. 2 oz.	76"	91"	91"	61"	6'	Double Mummy
4 lbs. 8 oz.	72"	66"	66"	46"	6'	Mummy
3 lbs. 4 oz.	72"	66"	66"	46"	6'	Mummy
5 lbs.	75"	72"	72"	72"	6' 1"	Rectangular
7 lbs.	84"	106"	106"	106"	6' 3"	Double Rectangle

ZIPPER TYPE AND LENGTH	CHANNEL TYPE AND SIZE	CHANNEL ARRANGEMENT	DIFFERENTIAL
63″ two way #10	8″ V Channels	Transverse	Yes
63″ two way #10	8″ V Channels	Transverse	Yes
63″ two way #10	10″ V Channels	Transverse	Yes
63″ two way #10	12″ V Channels	Transverse	Yes
40″ one way # 5	8″ Box Channels	Transverse	Yes
104″ one way # 5	8″ Box Channels	Transverse	Yes
104″ one way # 5	8″ Box Channels	Transverse	Yes
70″ Nylon	V Channels	Transverse	No
70″ Nylon	Slant Box Channels	Transverse	Yes
70″ Nylon	Slant Box Channels	Transverse	Yes
70″ Nylon	Slant Box Channels	Transverse	No
99″ Nylon	Slant Box Channels	Transverse	No
99″ Nylon	Slant Box Channels	Transverse	No
99″ Nylon	Stitch Through	Quilt Pattern	No
99″ Nylon	Stitch Through	Transverse	No
44″ Nylon	Box Channels	Transverse	Yes
44″ Nylon	Box Channels	Transverse	Yes
24″ Center Metal	Box Channels	Chevron	Yes
24″ Center Metal	Box Channels	Chevron	Yes
24″ Center Metal	Box Channels	Chevron	Yes
24″ Center Metal	Box Channels	Chevron	Yes
107″ Metal	Laminated Channels	Longitudinal	No
102″ Metal	Stitch Through	Longitudinal	No
70″ Nylon #10	6″ Slant Box Channels	Transverse	No
70″ Nylon #10	6″ V Channels	Transverse	No
70″ Nylon #10	6″ V Channels	Transverse	No
70″ Nylon #10	6″ V Channels	Transverse	No
70″ Nylon #10	Slant Box Channels	Transverse	No
72″ Nylon #10	Slant Box Channels	Transverse	No
95″ Metal	7″ V Channels	Longitudinal	No
72″ Metal	7″ V Channels	Transverse	No
108″ Metal	7″ V Channels	Longitudinal	No
137″ Metal	7″ V Channels	Longitudinal	No

ROLLED SIZE	COLOR	SHELL AND LINER	PRICE
24x10	Orange	Nylon	$120.00
22x9	Blue	Nylon	92.50
20x8	Gold	Nylon	78.50
24x8	Green	Nylon	82.50
18x9	Red	Nylon	—
18x9	Red	Nylon	—
18x9	Blue	Nylon	55.00
	Blue, orange, gold	Ripstop Nylon	$ 75.00
	Blue, orange, gold	Ripstop Nylon	95.00
	Blue, orange, gold	Ripstop Nylon	85.00
	Blue, orange	Ripstop Nylon	110.00
	Blue, green, red	Nylon Taffeta	95.00
	Blue, green, red	Nylon Taffeta	75.00
	Green	Nylon Taffeta	58.00
	Green	Nylon Taffeta	35.00
22x9	Blue	Ripstop Nylon	$ 94.00
22x10	Blue	Ripstop Nylon	145.00
18x11	Olive Drab	Cotton	$ 74.80
17x9	Olive Drab	Cotton	65.00
19x9	Blue	Cotton	61.25
16x8	Blue	Cotton	44.75
18x11	Green	Cotton	33.50
17x11	Green	Cotton	21.50
18x10	Blue	Ripstop Nylon	$ 95.00
18x10	Blue	Ripstop Nylon	115.00
18x10	Blue	Ripstop Nylon	140.00
18x11	Blue	Ripstop Nylon	165.00
18x10	Blue	Ripstop Nylon	120.00
18x12	Blue	Ripstop Nylon	145.00
16x7	Green	Cotton	$ 67.95
16x7	Blue, red	Ripstop Nylon	80.50
17x8	Green	Cotton	62.00
18x10	Green	Cotton	87.95

Sleeping Bags

	MINIMUM TEMP	TOP LOFT	FILLING
SIERRA DESIGNS			
Omni, Regular	20°	3″	2⅜ lbs. Goose Down
Omni, Large	20°	3″	2½ lbs. Goose Down
100 Superlight, Large	10°	3¼″	1¾ lbs. Goose Down
100 Superlight, XL	10°	3¼″	2 lbs. Goose Down
200 Perfect, Large	0°	3½″	2⅜ lbs. Goose Down
200 Perfect, XL	0°	3½″	2⅝ lbs. Goose Down
300 Expedition, Large	−25°	4½″	2⅞ lbs. Goose Down
300 Expedition, XL	−25°	4½″	3¼ lbs. Goose Down
Double Mummy	5°	3¼″	3⅜ lbs. Goose Down
NORTH FACE			
Minimog, Regular	20°	3″	2¼ lbs. Duck Down
Minimog, Large	20°	3″	2⅜ lbs. Duck Down
Super Light, Regular	10°	3¼″	1½ lbs. Goose Down
Super Light, Large	10°	3¼″	1⅝ lbs. Goose Down
Unimog, Regular	5°	3½″	2¼ lbs. Goose Down
Unimog, Large	5°	3½″	2⅜ lbs. Goose Down
Ibex, Regular	0°	3¾″	2⅜ lbs. Goose Down
Ibex, Large	0°	3¾″	2⅗ lbs. Goose Down
North Face, Regular	−30°	4¾″	3 lbs. Goose Down
North Face, Large	−30°	4¾″	3¼ lbs. Goose Down
OCATE			
Standard, Small	− 5°	1″	Poly Foam
Standard, Medium	− 5°	1″	Poly Foam
Standard, Large	− 5°	1″	Poly Foam
Expedition, Medium	−20°	1½″	Poly Foam
Expedition, Large	−20°	1½″	Poly Foam
BLACKS			
Icecap, Large	0°		2¼ lbs. Goose Down
Icecap, Medium	0°		2 lbs. Goose Down
Summit	0°		2⅝ lbs. Goose Down
Polar	0°		2½ lbs. Goose Down
Norland, Large	5°		2 lbs. Goose Down
Norland, Standard	5°		1½ lbs. Goose Down
Icelandic	5°		1⅜ lbs. Goose Down
Trail, Extra Large	0°		2½ lbs. Goose Down
Trail, Large	10°		1½ lbs. Goose Down
THAW (FROM KELTY)			
Icelander	10°		3½ lbs. Dacron
RECREATIONAL EQUIPMENT			
Bivouac	30°	1½″	1½ lbs. Goose Down
Mount Etna	30°	1½″	1 lb. Goose Down
ANTARCTIC IMPORTS			
Antarctica	0°	2¼″	2¾ lbs. Goose Down
Antarctica Mummy	0°	2¼″	2½ lbs. Goose Down

TOTAL WEIGHT	LENGTH	SHOULDER	HIP	FOOT	FOR PEOPLE	BAG SHAPE
4 lbs.	75"	64"	62"	46"	6'	Semi-Rectangle
4 lbs. 4 oz.	81"	64"	62"	46"	6' 4"	Semi-Rectangle
3 lbs.	72"	56"	53"	34"	6'	Narrow Mummy
3 lbs. 6 oz.	79"	56"	53"	34"	6' 7"	Narrow Mummy
4 lbs.	72"	62"	58"	40"	6'	Mummy
3 lbs. 6 oz.	79"	62"	58"	40"	6' 7"	Mummy
4 lbs. 12 oz.	72"	62"	58"	40"	6'	Mummy
5 lbs. 4 oz.	79"	62"	58"	40"	6' 7"	Mummy
6 lbs.	75"	98"	98"	62"	6' 2"	Double Mummy
3 lbs. 12 oz.	79"	62"	53"	46"	6' 2"	Semi-Rectangle
4 lbs.	85"	62"	53"	46"	6' 4"	Semi-Rectangle
3 lbs.	74"	58"	52"	38"	6'	Mummy
3 lbs. 2 oz.	79"	60"	52"	38"	6' 4"	Mummy
3 lbs. 12 oz.	79"	62"	53"	46"	6' 2"	Semi-Rectangle
4 lbs.	85"	62"	53"	46"	6' 4"	Semi-Rectangle
3 lbs. 14 oz.	74"	62"	56"	40"	6'	Mummy
4 lbs. 2 oz.	81"	62"	56"	40"	6' 6"	Mummy
4 lbs. 8 oz.	74"	62"	54"	40"	6'	Mummy
4 lbs. 12 oz.	80"	62"	54"	40"	6' 6"	Mummy
4 lbs.	62"				5' 6"	Mummy
4 lbs. 4 oz.	76"				6' 2"	Mummy
4 lbs. 8 oz.	80"				7'	Mummy
6 lbs.	74"				6'	Mummy
6 lbs. 8 oz.	80"				7'	Mummy
3 lbs. 8 oz.	77"	60"	60"	48"	6' 1"	Semi-Rectangular
3 lbs.	72"	54"	54"	44"	6'	Semi-Rectangular
4 lbs. 8 oz.	73"	66"	66"	42"	6'	Mummy
5 lbs.	82"	66"	66"	42"	6' 2"	Mummy
4 lbs.	78"	50"	66"	50"	6' 1"	Semi-Rectangular
3 lbs. 8 oz.	78"	66"	66"	38"	6' 1"	Semi-Rectangular
4 lbs.	78"	66"	66"	38"	6' 1"	Semi-Rectangular
5 lbs. 8 oz.	84"	60"	72"	60"	6' 2	Semi-Rectangular
4 lbs. 8 oz.	78"	50"	66"	50"	6' 1"	Semi-Rectangular
5 lbs. 10 oz.	74"	68"	60"	40"	6'	Mummy
2 lbs. 4 oz.	80"	54"	54"	40"	6' 2"	Mummy
2 lbs. 2 oz.	78"	66"	66"	42"	6' 1"	Semi-Rectangular
5 lbs.	75"	66"	66"	66"	6' 2"	Rectangular
4 lbs. 4 oz.	85"	60"	54"	40"	6' 2"	Mummy

ZIPPER TYPE AND LENGTH	CHANNEL TYPE AND SIZE	CHANNEL ARRANGEMENT	DIFFERENTIAL
103" Nylon #7	6" Box Channels	Transverse	Yes
109" Nylon #7	6" Box Channels	Transverse	Yes
70" Nylon #7	6" Box Channels	Transverse	Yes
70" Nylon #7	6" Box Channels	Transverse	Yes
70" Nylon #7	6" Box Channels	Transverse	Yes
70" Nylon #7	6" Box Channels	Transverse	Yes
70" Nylon #7	6" V Channels	Transverse	Yes
70" Nylon #7	6" V Channels	Transverse	Yes
70" Nylon #7	6" Box Channels	Transverse	Yes
100" Nylon #10	Box Channels	Transverse	Yes
106" Nylon #10	Box Channels	Transverse	Yes
70" Nylon #10	Box Channels	Transverse	Yes
70" Nylon #10	Box Channels	Transverse	Yes
100" Nylon #10	Box Channels	Transverse	Yes
106" Nylon #10	Box Channels	Transverse	Yes
70" Nylon #10	Box Channels	Transverse	Yes
70" Nylon #10	Box Channels	Transverse	Yes
70" Nylon #10	Box Channels	Transverse	Yes
70" Nylon #10	Box Channels	Transverse	Yes
None	None	None	Yes
None	None	None	Yes
None	None	None	Yes
None	None	None	Yes
None	None	None	Yes
77" Metal	V Channels	Transverse	Yes
72" Metal	V Channels	Transverse	Yes
72" Metal	V Channels	Transverse	No
82" Metal	8" Box Channels	Transverse	No
78" Nylon	V Channels	Transverse	Yes
78" Nylon	V Channels	Transverse	Yes
28" Metal	Box Channels	Transverse	No
28" Metal	Box Channels	Transverse	No
28" Metal	Box Channels	Transverse	No
18" Metal	Laminated	Transverse	No
40" Metal	Box Channels	Transverse	No
None	Stitched Through	Transverse	No
108" Metal	4" Box Channels	Chevron	Yes
30" Metal	4" Box Channels	Chevron	Yes

ROLLED SIZE	COLOR	SHELL AND LINER	PRICE
	Blue	Ripstop Nylon	$ 92.00
	Blue	Ripstop Nylon	97.00
	Blue, red	Ripstop Nylon	84.00
	Blue, red	Ripstop Nylon	90.00
	Blue, orange	Ripstop Nylon	98.00
	Blue, orange	Ripstop Nylon	104.00
	Blue, red	Ripstop Nylon	120.00
	Blue, red	Ripstop Nylon	130.00
	Blue	Ripstop Nylon	140.00
	Blue, green	Ripstop Nylon	$ 72.50
	Blue, green	Ripstop Nylon	75.00
	Blue, green, orange	Ripstop Nylon	78.00
	Blue, green, orange	Ripstop Nylon	82.00
	Blue, green, orange	Ripstop Nylon	94.00
	Blue, green, orange	Ripstop Nylon	98.00
	Blue, orange	Ripstop Nylon	97.50
	Blue, orange	Ripstop Nylon	102.50
	Gold	Ripstop Nylon	135.00
	Gold	Ripstop Nylon	140.00
15x8			$ 53.60
16x9			55.00
16x9			59.00
18x11			75.00
19x12			84.00
16x8	Blue		$ 99.95
14x8	Blue		89.95
16x8	Blue		99.95
18x9	Fawn, sky		77.50
16x9	Blue		94.50
14x8	Blue		85.00
15x8	Blue, sky	Cotton	55.95
18x9	Fawn, sky	Cotton	79.95
17x8	Fawn, sky	Cotton	64.50
16x10	Blue, green		$ 38.95
14x7	Red		$ 49.95
15x8	Red		34.85
12x9	Blue		$ 47.00
12x9	Blue		46.00

262

LIGHTWEIGHT FOODS

The backpacker and hiker are familiar with a wide range of equipment and techniques that the motorcyclist and bicyclist can use. But much of what has been developed for the pedestrian must be adapted for the cyclist. The two wheel camper is in a different situation with regard to food supply than is the backpacker. He is on the road and has the opportunity to buy fresh food stuffs daily. The backpacker's reason for walking may well be to avoid just such opportunities, but he and the biker have in common many problems involving waste, weight, bulk, and spoilage when it comes to food. And, of course, it's always difficult to carry tempting meals when you limit how much you carry and how often you replenish your supply. Modern backpacking techniques have improved the art of cooking to the point that a lot can be learned from the solutions that have been found.

Much of what you need to cook you use only a little of each meal so you carry it. What's more it is just these things, which often make the difference in taste. Working out how much and what you will buy along the road, and what you'll need to supplement and season it is a reasonably simple but valuable technique. A lot depends on what sort of tour you are interested in. 'Touring' means, literally, riding from town to town and staying in motels or inns and eating in restaurants. Camping is another thing entirely. Obviously, you can do some of both and have to plan accordingly.

If you want to be quite lost from sources of supply for some time, then you have to carry a considerable amount of food with you. Similarly, if you're going to areas where particular foods are part of the trip, then plan to take advantage of them. In Maine, lobster and steamers are excellent fare if you can afford them.

Any food you're going to carry, regardless of what proportion of your diet it will fill, has to be light and not spoil easily. Modern backpackers rely heavily on freeze-dried foods. The cyclist needn't restrict himself so exclusively to them as he is certainly not as limited as a wilderness walker. But their advantages are many and ought to be carefully considered.

Dehydrating foods, especially freeze-drying them, is a sensitive process and as a result the products are expensive. But, the advantages in prepackaging convenience allowed by their ability to keep indefinitely without refrigeration and their low bulk and weight characteristics make them a valuable food for touring. They aren't as good tasting as fresh food, of course. But, they're not as bad as you'd think. In fact, they are generally on a par with frozen food. Properly used, modern freeze-dries retain much of the taste and consistency of fresh goods.

By using dehydrates, a good deal of what you'll eat can be premixed, repackaged in polyethylene bags, labeled and sorted ahead of time and thus more simply prepared on the road. The plastic containers for such packaging are available from nearly every camping retailer in all sizes. It's enough to say a single dish can be stored in the smallest plastic bags, the pint and quart sizes, and the whole collection can then be put in laundry-sized double bags and sealed off from the rest of the pack. Further division into daily supplies can also be made. Plastic bottles, canteens, and jars, as well, can be useful in prepackaging.

The extreme convenience of these nonperishable foods comes on a really long, cross-country tour in which you don't want to carry all the food and equipment you will need. Some of the stuff can simply be mailed ahead general delivery. A week's supplies can be sent to a number of towns and you can quickly and easily pick them up as you pass through. Or one evening before the trip you can have the whole thing laid out in accurate measure and arrange a reasonably flexible diet. You can scatter dishes around and combine them on the road as whim dictates or you can set up a dietary lockstep for every moment of the trip. Whichever suits your taste. But, regardless of how you arrange your food supply, premixing of some sort is a boon in time and hassle once you're on the road.

You can buy dehydrates premixed and sorted for you. You can even get a full day's food, three meals, for four people prepackaged in one convenient box. But, you can also go through the small amount of work necessary to mix these foods yourself. The equipment you'll need to prepare your meals in advance is easily had. The only articles you won't find in any kitchen are a postal scale for weighing the freeze dried foods, a felt tip pen to label things, and an assortment of polyethylene bags, bottles and thirty-five millimeter film cans.

Basic combinations to suit taste, like whole and skim milk powder or cocoa and milk powder, are only the beginning. Dry seasonings can be added to dry main dishes ahead of time and a complete dehydrated stew can be packed in a bag with its cooking instructions. Or, those particular seasoning ingredients for a dish, the main part of which will be bought on the road, can be packaged and added when you make camp.

Choosing from among the many specialty manufacturers of these foods isn't easy. They all make a number of different dishes and combinations of dishes. One useful distinction, however, is that between standard dehydrating processes and freeze drying.

Air drying or vacuum dehydrating is accomplished by placing foods in the air or in a vacuum chamber until its water content has been evaporated. The water evaporating to the surface of the food carries with it salts and some proteins, and the concentration of these substances at the surface produces a tough, sometimes even hard layer.

Freeze-drying is a particular dehydrating process. It involves removing water from *frozen* foods in a vacuum. Mineral salts and proteins do not move to the surface and a more stable distribution results. The foods remain about the same size, shape, and flavor and are approximately ¼ their original weight. Rehydrating is quicker because there is no tough outer layer, and the foods generally taste better. Freeze-dried foods cost a little more because of the added steps in the process and the expense of freezing the original foods.

Dehydrated foods, available in small, simple units, are manufactured by a number of firms. There is a considerable amount of product overlapping among the camping food companies. The list that is included in the text is intended to give you some idea of what's available and how it is packaged. This listing has been compiled from foods that you can order both from mail-order supply houses that handle other kinds of camping supplies and those that you can obtain direct from the manufacturer. Buying through a retailer may be the simplest way since he will usually carry a number of different manufacturers' products and so make ordering all you need at one time much easier. However, addresses for further information are given for both manufacturers and retailers that have particularly large selections of dehydrates. There are, certainly, a number of both varieties of suppliers that aren't mentioned.

Modern dehydrates are also packaged in three and four course meals for two-, four-, or eight-man groups. Some go so far as to provide a full day's menu, complete with dessert, in one small cardboard box. This sort of diet is designed for the backpacking family, mountain group, and hunting or fishing party. It has been adapted by a number of companies who got involved in dehydrating foods during the heyday of fallout shelters and the scramble to fill them with nonperishable foods. These also make good peacetime emergency food units. Due to the stability of freeze-dries, they can be stored for long periods in the trunks of cars or in planes without refrigeration. But, to limit one's diet to such menus when mobility is available is stupid. Although dehydrates have improved there is no reason to restrict yourself to such relatively bland fare for days on end. For the curious, here's a sample of this kind of menu —a full day's food supply from Kamp Pack:

---

4 PERSON PACK
12 FULL MEALS
$10.75

MENU NO. 5

8 PERSON PACK
24 FULL MEALS
$19.20

BREAKFAST
INSTANT ZOOM CEREAL with MILK, SUGAR and FRUIT
SCRAMBLED EGGS DE LUXE
DE LUXE CORN BREAD
GOLDEN CLEAR NO STICK
HOT CHOCOLATE

CHOICE OF HOT OR COLD LUNCH

HOT LUNCH	COLD LUNCH
CAMPERS STEW	TUNA FISH SALAD SPREAD
PILOT BISCUITS	CHEESE and CRACKERS
FRUIT SAUCE MIX	PILOT BISCUITS
FRUIT PUNCH	FRUIT PUNCH

DINNER
TOMATO NOODLE SOUP
TRAIL STEW
HOT BISCUITS
INSTANT PUDDING
CHOCOLATE MILK SHAKE

It's comforting to know that really bad foods won't dehydrate properly. As a result, most of the reputable processors of these foods choose their raw materials very carefully. Freeze-dries also remain very high in nutritional value for years, so long as they're kept from water. But, they are not better, and are sometimes worse, than the food that originally went into them. Most of the fresh foods that are the raw material for the freeze-drying process are the products of chemical sprays, contain sulphur and nitrate additives and, also, food coloring and stabilizers. Some companies put more synthetic additives into their foods than others and if you're interested, you can simply compare the labels. There are a few firms growing or buying organic foods, which are then dried and preserved without the use of chemicals:

Chico San
1262 Humbolt Avenue
Chico, California 95926

Sturdee Health Products
238 Livingston Street
Brooklyn, New York

A few of the larger retailers with good selections of conventional and freeze-dried foods are listed below. The brands of dehydrated foods which they carry are also given. Their mailing addresses can be found in the appendix of camping suppliers' guides.

Recreational Equipment, Inc.
Wilson, Seidel, Richmoor, Mountain House, Tea Kettle, and a line of their own packaged foods, assorted cereals and candies.

Eastern Mountain Sports
Wilson, Richmoor, and Trail Chef.

The Smilie Company
One of the largest lines including nearly all those given in the listing.

Camp and Trail Outfitters
Chuck Wagon, Trail Chef, Wilson, and an assortment of their own foods.

You can also buy directly from a number of manufacturers:

Kisky Foods
1829 Northeast Alberta Street
Portland, Oregon 97211

Kamp Pack
Bernard Foods, Inc.
1125 Harley Avenue
Box 1497
Evanston, Illinois 60204

Camplite
40 East 2430 South
Salt Lake City, Utah 84115

S. Gumpert Co.,
812 Jersey Avenue
Jersey City, New Jersey 07302

Trail Chef
1109 South Wall Street
Los Angeles, California 90015

Dri-Lite Foods
11333 Atlantic Avenue
Lunwood, California 90264

Chuck Wagon Foods
175 Oak Street
Newtown, Massachusetts 02164

Richmoor Corporation
Box 2728
Van Nuys, California 91404

Stow Away Products
103 Ripley Road
Cohasset, Massachusetts 02025

BREAKFAST FOODS

Food	Brand	Net Weight		Servings	Price
Powdered Whole Eggs One tablespoon equals an egg	Hirsch	8	ounces	16	$1.80
Scrambled Egg Mix	DriLite	3½	ounces	4	.75
Scrambled Egg with Ham With bits of freeze-dried ham	Wilson	2¾	ounces	2	1.40
Western Omelette With onions and peppers	Richmoor	4½	ounces	4	1.15
Cheese Omelette	Trail Chef	5¾	ounces	4	1.25
Pancake Mix	Richmoor	12	ounces	4	.50
Pancake Syrup Mix	Seidel	9	ounces	4	.45
Buttermilk Pancake Mix	Seidel	11	ounces	4	.52
Blueberry Syrup Mix	Richmoor	6½	ounces	4	.40

VEGETABLE DISHES

Food	Brand	Net Weight		Servings	Price
Peas (freeze-dried)	Wilson	16	ounces		3.75
Mushrooms (freeze-dried)	Wilson	3½	ounces		6.50
Corn (freeze-dried)	Richmoor	2¼	ounces	4	.70
Green Beans (freeze-dried)	Richmoor	1	ounce	4	.70
Peas and Carrots	Richmoor	2¾	ounces	4	.75
Spanish Rice	Kamp Pack	9½	ounces		1.02
Precooked Rice	Minute	7	ounces	6	.35
Hashed Brown Potatoes	Trail Chef	4	ounces	4	.65
Mashed Potatoes Au Gratin	Trail Chef	4	ounces	4	.50
Vegetable Mix	Smilie	3	ounces	4	.60

DINNER DISHES

Diced Ham Precooked, freeze-dried	Wilson	1	ounce	2	.75
Pork Chops No bones, freeze-dried	Wilson	2	ounces	2	1.60
Beef Steaks Two per can	Wilson	2	ounces	2	2.60
Chicken (freeze-dried)	Richmoor	1¼	ounces		1.35
Beef (freeze-dried)	Richmoor	1¼	ounces		1.20
Ham (freeze-dried)	Richmoor	1¼	ounces		1.55

MIXED DINNERS

Vegetable-Beef Stew	Richmoor	8¾	ounces	4	2.60
Chili Con Carne with Beef	Richmoor	12½	ounces	4	2.25
Beef Stroganoff with Noodles	Richmoor	12¾	ounces	4	2.40
Chicken A La King	Richmoor	6½	ounces	4	1.65
Turkey Supreme with Noodles	Richmoor	13¼	ounces	4	2.35
Beef Taco Comida	Richmoor	9	ounces	4	2.20
Shrimp Creole	Richmoor	10¾	ounces	4	2.60
Corned Beef	Libby	7	ounces	4	.49
Freeze-dried Shrimp Contains 25 large shrimp	Oregon F.D.	1	ounce	2	2.20

FRUITS AND SALADS

Fig Slices	Smilie	5	ounces	4	.50
Peach Nuggets	Smilie	3	ounces	4	.65
Instant Apple Wedges	Smilie	3	ounces	4	.55
Instant Applesauce	Smilie	5	ounces	4	.75
Mixed Fruit	Smilie	4	ounces	4	.75
Pear Slices	Smilie	4	ounces	4	.65
Strawberry Slices	Oregon F.D.	1	ounce	4	1.00
Raisins	Sunmaid	9	ounces	6	.30
Fruit Cocktail	Richmoor	6	ounces	6	.90
Tuna Salad	Trail Chef	3⅜	ounces	4	1.83
Chicken Salad	Trail Chef	3½	ounces	4	1.50
Egg Salad	Trail Chef	3⅞	ounces	4	1.25

Camping Foods That Aren't Dehydrates

Campers are inclined to look for foods designed and marketed for their use and the freeze-dried foods certainly fill the bill. But, foods that happen to suit the camping cyclist that aren't necessarily advertised as such can be had from a number of sources.

Since water is the critically heavy part of foods, many are dehydrated by expensive processes. Just as good are characteristically dry foods like spaghetti, rice and oatmeal. Much cheaper, as well, are those which are dried by much simpler processes or those which have only some of their natural water removed like prunes, apricots, and raisins.

You can also look for foods that are normally dry and which are especially high in nutritional value. This will allow you to get more food from less bulk and weight. The most obvious source of these foods is the organic and health food stores that are cropping up all over the place. High protein foods and vitamin supplements abound on their shelves. Simply because they're better foods, they supply more of what you need and so take less room on your bike.

Mail-order services that don't require bulk orders are scarce in this line, but most stores either stock what you'd like or can be moved to get it. Many items associated with health food distributors can also be found in grocery stores. It's really hard to pick particular items from these lines, but some that I like and that seem to be practical are suggested below. The only mail-order house which handles small unit sales that I know anything about is:

> Walnut Acres Mill and Store
> Penns Creek, Pennsylvania 17862

Foods:

Granolas: Crunchy, Hi Protein, Honey Almond Crunch, natural Swiss types and Vita-grains with nuts are all common. 1 pound, 69¢, 3 pounds $1.85.

Quaker's Instant Oatmeal: Easy and quick to prepare, this old favorite can be found at any grocery store. With any kind of oatmeal some brown sugar helps. 10 ounces, 10 packets, 39¢.

McCann's Finest Oatmeal: Great oatmeal, but less convenient than the instants. One cup of raw oatmeal cooks to about four or five cups. 28 ounces, $1.39.

Familia Swiss Breakfast: A very sweet, organically grown cereal, fruit, and almond mixture that has a high protein content. High wheat germ and oat proportions. 2½ ounces, 25¢; 2 pounds, $1.99.

Fini Swiss Muesli Cereal: Like Familia but with dried skim milk added. Prices are about the same as those for Familia.

Wheat Germ: A good, high protein addition to any cereal or salad. Be sure to buy the toasted variety as untoasted wheat germ will go rancid without refrigeration. 12 ounces, 85¢.

Dried fruits make a good, odd moment filler or

an able addition to breakfast. Apples are especially light. 1 pound, 85¢. Raisins are bulk for the troubled system not taking the change of life kindly. They are also a very concentrated food: 1 pound, 45¢. Apricots, too: 1 pound, $1.10.

Swift's Canned Bacon: Not bad tasting, though not so good as regular bacon since much of the taste is lost when its fats are removed. Swift's is twice as heavy as 'bacon bars' of dried, prefried bacon sold at mountain and backpacking stores but tastes good. If you usually eat bacon in the morning, buy some fresh the night before and eat it all. Eating it all, of course, is the problem if you are alone or in a small group. Hence, this entry on canned bacon.

Beef Jerky: Pretty good as an addition to soups and stews. It isn't hard to prepare and by doing so you can make a very good supply with better meat and personally preferred seasonings. Very lean, top round or better beef is best, but be sure to trim any fat meticulously. Slice it in baconlike strips about ¼ inch thick and pound the strips as thin as possible. Season it as you will but at least salt the meat.

Lower the beef into boiling, very salty water with whatever screened basket is handy. Less than half a minute will have the beef whitened a bit and the strips should be drained.

Think up a way to hang the beef strips to dry and cover them tightly enough to keep the flies off with cheese cloth. Hang them outside in a sunny, safe place for five hot days. Air circulation will help the drying process and rain will ruin it so cover the jerky only when necessary.

When they're dark and brittle the strips of jerky are done and can be kept in plastic bags indefinitely.

A Cookbook for the Road

Working with dehydrates over a fire or backpacking stove isn't difficult so long as you follow the directions that come with each package. Similarly, it's pretty easy to invent your own recipes. All you need do is compare the instructions and reconstituted volumes of dried foods with the amounts of regular food called for in the recipes of any cookbook. Test a small amount of such a conversion before you mix up a batch of it and head out.

It's generally cheaper and usually better tasting to buy in bulk and repackage dehydrates yourself. You can also put together combinations that you prefer this way. What you find here are some standard suggestions that relate to premixing and on the road cooking. If you carefully premix and package and are equally careful about your preparation you can enjoy some tasty combinations that are very portable and won't spoil in the summer heat. There's nothing tricky about it: when in doubt, add to any stew anything you like.

Kitchen Suggestions

Cooking time increases at higher altitudes and extra water may have to be added during the process. To hold evaporation to a minimum, cover your pots. A longer period of presoaking will make reconstituted dehydrates cook faster.

When simmering foods, or if instructions call for boiling, do so over low heat. Rapid boiling is not best for dehydrates and the flavor of the food improves with slow cooking.

Presoaking is more effective in warm water. Dehydrates generally require thirty minutes of presoaking, but freeze-dries need only about five minutes. When reconstituting vegetables, beef, or chicken add a little wine and seasoning to the water in advance of cooking.

Margarine keeps better than butter and for cooking, vegetable oil is still more convenient.

Mark the outside of pots at measuring points.

Applying a thin coating of soap to the outside of pots will keep campfire soot from sticking and a quick rinse will clean the pot.

As for the inside of pots and pans, Teflon pans are accessible and you can also get do-it-yourself Teflon sprays. Also available from most camping suppliers is a pan coating called 'Vegalene.' Used sparingly, it won't affect foods but prevents them from sticking to the pan.

The makers of 'Camplite' foods suggest a variety of bread and muffin cooking techniques:

Gingerbread, cornbread and date bran muffin mixes can be prepared in a variety of ways. To bake them, you can use a covered skillet, a foil or reflector oven, two foil pie tins wrapped together with aluminum foil or even aluminum foil shaped to substitute for a baking container. You can make delicious "cakes" simply by thinning the batter with extra liquid and cooking them as you would pancakes. To make drop biscuits or spoon bread, prepare as you would for baking, but instead of pouring the batter into the pan, drop it in a spoonful at a time. Or prepare 'bread on a stick' by adding less water to the batter, keeping it thick enough to wrap around the end of a stick.

When dividing bags of dehydrated food, remember to add water in proportion to the food used.

Dehydrates increase in volume when reconstituted from three to four times, but freeze-dried foods generally remain about the same size.

Prepared stews generally contain more starch than meat. Adding freeze-dried meat to the package is a good idea and when cooking using some margarine will also improve the flavor.

Recipes

This first series of recipes can be measured at home, packaged, and mailed ahead. The dried foods that go into them will not spoil and are very light and compact. Any liquids that are called for can be bottled in the smallest of mountaineering supplier's plastic bottles and then mailed as well.

You will probably find that certain amounts of seasoning, or even of unusual additions to standard dishes that are suggested here, do not suit your tastes. Some, I hope, will. Remember that you can translate any standard cookbook recipe that you do like into freeze-dried equivalents without too much trouble. You can also buy a couple of the dehydrated foods cookbooks mentioned earlier and make changes to taste in their recipes. Going to this trouble before you leave is easy, will save a lot of time and provide better meals once you're on the road.

PANCAKES: Pancake mixes give directions. What follows is a list of pleasing variations.

pancake mix	7 ounces
powdered eggs	3 ounces
powdered milk	2 ounces
water	1½ ounces
margarine	4 ounces
plus:	
vacuum dried fruit	¼ cup
nutmeg	¼ teaspoon
or:	
dried lemon and orange rind (diced)	1 square inch each
vanilla	½ teaspoon
cognac	1 teaspoon

Eat pancakes with margarine, jam or cinnamon or both.

COLE SLAW:

cabbage or lettuce flakes	2 ounces
apples, pineapples, walnuts	½ cup
sour cream	3 ounces
dill weed	½ teaspoon
lemon juice or wine	1 tablespoon
salt	

SPINACH:

water	5 cups
spinach flakes	2½ cups
margarine	1 ounce
onion flakes	1 teaspoon
or:	
powdered milk	2 tablespoons
flour	1 tablespoon
nutmeg	some

A SAUCE FOR PEAS, BEANS, AND CORN:

margarine	2 tablespoons
flour	2 tablespoons
water	1 cup
powdered milk	3 ounces
salt and paprika	
or:	

A tablespoon or two of onion or pepper flakes or both.

MASHED POTATOES:

water	4 cups
margarine	2 ounces
dehydrated potatoes	7 ounces
powdered milk	½ cup
powdered egg	1 ounce

or:

You can try 3 cups of water and 1 cup of beer instead of the 4 cups of water.

CURRY SAUCE:

water	1 cup
flour	2 tablespoons
margarine	2 tablespoons
powdered milk	3 ounces
onion flakes	1 tablespoon
curry powder	2 teaspoons
paprika	⅛ teaspoon
coriander or ginger	1 teaspoon
raisins	
walnuts	¼ cup altogether
almonds	

You can mix this with hamburgers to keep them from being hamburgers or you can reconstitute freeze-dried shrimp, boil them, and serve them with curry over rice.

CHUTNEY:

dehydrated mixed fruit	6 ounces
water	3 cups
onion flakes	1 ounce
allspice	¼ teaspoon
garlic powder	½ teaspoon
ginger powder	½ teaspoon
cinnamon stick	1
sugar (brown if possible)	½ cup
dry mustard	1 tablespoon

Serve curry and chutney over rice with shrimp. Amazing.

The following are an odd combination of good things to eat that are easy to prepare on the road. They are generally very simple and nutritious. The recipe for salted soybeans is intended to be followed at home to prepare a good snack. You may prefer simply buying some; you can get them in health foods stores. They are made by Sovec, Inc. and are sold as 'Nature Nuggets.' Roasted soybeans are 36% protein and delicious.

SALTED SOYBEANS:

Wash and soak the dry beans overnight; then drain and spread them out at room temperature until the surface is dry. Fry a few at a time in deep fat (with garlic or onion if you like) at 350° F for 8 to 10 minutes. Drain the beans on absorbent paper and sprinkle them with salt while they are still warm.

WOODSMAN'S COFFEE:

Add the egg shells from breakfast to the coffee grinds before brewing. Strain and lace the coffee with whiskey. Gives you a whole new outlook.

BROWN RICE:

water	2½ cups
rice	1 cup
salt	1 teaspoon

Salt the water. Bring it to a boil. Add the rice and boil hard, uncovered for 5 minutes. Lower the heat, cover, simmer for about 40 minutes. Do not uncover or stir. When rice is done all the water will have been absorbed and small 'air pockets' will have formed between the surface grains.

Barley and wheat berries can be prepared this way. Wheat berries are especially good mixed in with the rice because of their distinctive flavor and texture.

BASIC BULGHUR:

oil	2 tablespoons
bulghur	2 cups
hot water	4 cups

Heat the oil. Sauté the bulghur, making sure all grains are coated with oil. Add the water, cover tightly, and simmer gently for 15 minutes or until bulghur has absorbed all the liquid.

BUCKWHEAT GROATS:

Buckwheat groats	1 cup
stock or water	2 cups
salt	1 teaspoon

Boil 1 minute and then cover. Simmer over low heat for 12 to 15 minutes.

BOOKS ON TRAIL COOKERY

FOOD FOR KNAPSACKERS AND OTHER TRAIL TRAVELERS, by Hasse Bunnelle and Winnie Thomas, $1.95 from:

> The Sierra Club
> 250 West 57th Street
> New York, New York 10019

This is a small, durable little book from the Sierra Club series of 'Totebooks.' Designed to be brought along on the route, it will also serve well in helping your prepackaging freeze-dried menus before the trip. The book is directed towards backpackers who carry all their food with them, but, as part of a diet, the recipes included and equipment discussions are good.

BACKPACK COOKERY, by Ruth Dyer Mendenhall, La Siesta Press, $1.00.

Mendenhall's is only in part a dehydrates cookbook and covers a range of foods that can easily be picked up daily at local groceries. It's a tight little guide explaining a great deal about what to buy and how to package it for the road. These are cheap, good tasting recipes.

THE OUTDOOR COOK'S BIBLE, by Joseph D. Bates, Doubleday, $1.95.
Considered the authoritative work in the field, this book is heavy on old woodsman techniques and seems best for a hunting or fishing party that will have a base camp, mules to carry the gear, and a guide to do the cooking. It contains some excellent recipes though.

SOURDOUGH JACK'S COOKERY, by Mabee, $3.25.
This book is available from nearly every mountain supply company. It gives fifty-five recipes for sourdough-based bread, cookies, pancakes, etc., and comes with a batch of sourdough starter which will last indefinitely. From:

L. L. Bean
Cookbook and Starter: $4.00 postpaid.
Stoneware, Pot, and Starter: $2.50 postpaid.

AGRICULTURAL HANDBOOK NUMBER EIGHT: COMPOSITION OF FOODS, by Watt and Merrill, $2.00.
A really thorough handbook of food composition that you may find in large libraries but will otherwise have to buy from:

The Superintendent of Documents
U.S. Government Printing Office
Washington, D.C. 20402

THE IMPOVERISHED STUDENT'S BOOK OF COOKERY, DRINKERY, AND HOUSEKEEPERY, by Jay F. Rosenberg, Doubleday, $1.50.

CAMPING EQUIPMENT SUPPLIERS

This is a listing of some of the suppliers of camping equipment suitable to the needs of the touring cyclist. The first of the listings include backpacking and mountaineering specialists whose equipment is the lightest, generally the best made and so most efficient and always the most expensive. These dealers sell equipment quite often made by the same few first rate manufacturers. If you're not familiar with that equipment, buying through the mail can be difficult, so send for a number of different catalogues. The best of them have good, detailed photos and thorough descriptions. Even if you're going to the shop to buy, get the catalogue and study what's avilable before you go in to get your stuff. All the catalogues are free unless otherwise noted.

Alpine Designs
Box 3561
6185 East Arapahoe
Boulder, Colorado 80302

Alpine Hut
4725 30th Avenue North East
Seattle, Washington 98105

Alp Sport
Box 1081
3235 Prairie Avenue
Boulder, Colorado 80302

Antarctic Products, Ltd.
Box 223
Nelson, New Zealand

Arthur Ellis and Company
Dunedin, New Zealand

Eddie Bauer
1737 Airport Way South
Seattle, Washington 98134

Bishop's Ultimate Outdoor
Equipment
6804 Millwood Road
Bethesda, Maryland 20034

Bishop's is a tent manufacturer. Their mountaineering 'Ultimates' are certainly the best but are too much tent for the biker. Their smaller backpacking models have the same quality and many of the advantages of Blanchard design as have the expedition models. Good free catalogue.

Eastern Mountain Sports
1041 Commonwealth Avenue
Boston, Massachusetts 02215

The EMS catalogue is incredible. Nearly two hundred pages and a third color it is the quintessential camping wish book. Good descriptions and extraordinary tables are everywhere. They carry most of the highest quality equipment and you can get some idea of the stuff from this book of theirs no matter where you're going to buy. In short, light weight gear moves east.

Gerry Mountain Sports
Box 910
821 Pearl Street
Boulder, Colorado 80302

The Gerry division of Outdoor Sports Industries, makes fine lightweight gear. The equipment catalogue of Gerry equipment can be had through them:
5450 North Valley Highway
Denver, Colorado 80216

Gloy's
12 East 22nd Street
New York, New York 10010

EMS 71/72

Gloy's is a supplier of equipment to go with your bag, tent and pack. Pots, pans, stoves, tent pegs, and the like. Their catalogue is free.

Highland Outfitters
Box 121
3579 University Avenue
Riverside, California 92502

Himalayan Products
807 Ocean View Avenue
Monterey, California 93940
Basically pack bags of high quality. They also sell a couple of their own tents and sleeping bags though they're not exactly known for this end of their line.

Holubar Mountaineering
Box 7
1975 30th Street
Boulder, Colorado 80302
Holubar makes the best sleeping bags in the world. They've also got some good tent and down clothing but their designs are mountaineering-oriented. Because they put more into their sleeping bags than anybody else, the rap about bags in the catalogue doesn't leave anything left unsaid.

Kelty
1801 Victory Boulevard
Glendale, California 91201

The most famous of the pack makers doesn't make a variety of packs for bikers, but they have a good general catalogue.

Peter Limmer and Sons
Intervale, New Hampshire 03845
Limmer's is a small company selling good backpacking gear. They are most famous for their handcrafted custom-made boots.

Moor and Mountain
67 Main Street
Concord, Massachusetts 01742

Mountain Products
123 South Wenatchee
Wenatchee, Washington 98801

The North Face
308 Columbus Avenue
San Francisco, California 94133
Excellent equipment for the biker. The North Face doesn't make many things but what there is of it is great. Their catalogue is thin but the full length descriptions of each piece of equipment make it very interesting. They are now developing an injection moulded frame to replace tubular aluminum stays in walking packs.

MOOR & MOUNTAIN
Fall-Winter 1971

Recreation Equipment, Inc.
1525 11th Avenue
Seattle, Washington 98122
This is a cooperative that you have to join, for $1, in order to be able to choose from about as wide a selection of gear as is sold anywhere. They make some of it themselves and gather the rest from other manufacturers. They are less fussy about what they carry, but the effect is to make some serviceable stuff available at less than the going specialty rates.

Sierra Designs
Fourth and Addison Streets
Berkeley, California 94071
Excellent and superlight weight equipment. Theirs is a descriptive catalogue with good photos.

The Ski Hut
1615 University Avenue
Berkeley, California 94703
A large selection of excellent equipment. Their Trailwise stuff is very good and the catalogue has lots of clear color photos.

The Sport Chalet
Box 186
951 Foothill Boulevard
La Canada, California 91011

Stephenson's
23206 Hatteras Street
Woodland Hills, California 91364
Stephenson's makes Warmlite tents and sleeping bags. Both are radical in design, extraordinarily light weight and expensive. Their catalogue presents the arguments in favor of their stuff pretty well.

Swiss Ski Imports
559 Clay Street
San Francisco, California 94111

Universal Field Equipment
Mira Loma Space Center
Mira Loma, California 91752

The following are suppliers who are generally more economical though their equipment will rarely be as good as that found in specialty shops.

Alaska Sleeping Bag
13150 South West Dawson Way
Beaverton, Oregon 97005

Alpine Recreation
Box 54
Mount Vernon, New York 10552

L. L. Bean
Freeport, Maine 04032

Thomas Black and Sons
930 Ford Street
Ogdensburg, New York 13669

Camp and Trail Outfitters
112 Chambers Street
New York, New York 10007

Camp Trails
Box 14500
3920 West Clarendon Avenue
Phoenix, Arizona 85031

Eureka Tent and Awning
625 Conklin Road
Bingham, New York 13902

Don Gleason's Camper's Supply
9 Pearl Street
Northampton, Massachusetts 01060
    Catalogue costs 25¢

I. Goldberg
902 Chestnut Street
Philadelphia, Pennsylvania 19107
    Catalogue costs 35¢

H & H Surplus Center
305 West Baltimore Street
Baltimore, Maryland 21223

Herter's
Route 1
Waseca, Minnesota 56093
    Catalogue costs $1.00

Morsan
810 Route 17
Paramus, New Jersey 07652

Orvis
Manchester, Vermont 05254

The Smilie Company
575 Howard Street
San Francisco, California 94105
    Catalogue costs 10¢

Stow-A-Way Products
103 Ripley Road
Cohasset, Massachusetts 02025